AI FOR ENHANCING LIBRARY SERVICES

A GUIDE

Dr. Rajesh Rangappa Aldarthi
Prof. Manoj Kumar Sinha
Prof. Shantadevi T Akkarki

First Edition 2024

Published by Dr. Rajesh Rangappa Aldarthi, Prof. Manoj Kumar Sinha, Prof. Shantadevi T Akkarki

CONTENTS

INTRODUCTION

In this ever-evolving technological era, the impact of artificial intelligence (AI) is permeating various sectors, including library services. "AI for Enhancing Library Services: A Guide" is a comprehensive resource that delves into the profound implications and transformative possibilities of AI in the library service domain.

This guide aims to demystify the complex world of AI and illuminate how it can be harnessed to upgrade and streamline library services. It meticulously unravels the intricate relationship between AI and library services, providing a holistic viewpoint on how AI can revolutionize these services, thereby augmenting user experience and satisfaction.

Readers will gain a thorough understanding of the fundamental concepts of AI, its multifaceted applications, and the potential challenges of integrating AI into library services. This guide is designed to cater to a wide audience spectrum, from library professionals who wish to leverage AI for improving their services to students and researchers interested in the intersection of AI and library science.

The book unfolds with an exploration of the basic principles of AI, gradually moving towards its advanced features and how they can be adapted for library services. It provides practical insights into the successful implementation of AI in libraries, supported by real-world examples and case studies.

Moreover, the guide also delves into the ethical considerations and the potential pitfalls associated with the use of AI in library services. It encourages readers to critically assess the implications of AI, promoting a balanced and informed approach towards the adoption of AI in library services.

"AI for Enhancing Library Services: A Guide" is not just a theoretical exploration of AI's possibilities in library services. It is a practical tool, a roadmap for library professionals and enthusiasts to understand, adapt, and implement AI in their respective environments, thereby transforming the way library services are delivered.

By navigating through this guide, readers will be equipped with the knowledge and skills required to navigate the AI landscape in library services, shaping the future of libraries in the digital age.

Chapter 1: Introduction to AI in Library Services

Understanding AI

Delving into the world of artificial intelligence (AI) can seem like venturing into a labyrinth of complex algorithms and futuristic concepts. Yet, at its core, AI is simply about creating machines or systems that can perform tasks that would normally require human intelligence. This includes tasks such as understanding natural language, recognizing patterns, problem-solving, and learning from experience.

AI is essentially a multidisciplinary field that encompasses computer science, mathematics, cognitive psychology, and even philosophy. It seeks to create systems that can function independently, improving their performance based on the feedback they receive. This ability to learn and adapt is what sets AI apart from traditional computer programs.

There are two main categories of AI: narrow AI and general AI. Narrow AI, also known as weak AI, is designed to perform a specific task, such as voice recognition. These systems are prevalent in our daily lives, from Siri on our iPhones to recommendation algorithms on Netflix. Despite their seeming intelligence, these systems operate under a limited set of constraints and are only as smart as their programming allows.

On the other hand, general AI, also known as strong AI, is a system with generalized human cognitive abilities. When presented with an unfamiliar task, a strong AI system is capable of finding a solution without human intervention. While this concept is a staple of science fiction, it remains largely theoretical with current technology.

AI has the potential to revolutionize a multitude of industries, and libraries are no exception. Imagine a library where AI-powered robots assist with book retrieval or an intelligent system that can provide personalized reading recommendations based on a user's reading history and preferences. AI can also assist with digitization efforts, making it easier to preserve and access a library's vast collection of resources.

However, the integration of AI into library services is not without its challenges. Ethical considerations are paramount when dealing with AI. For instance, how do we ensure that AI systems respect user privacy and do not contribute to the digital divide? Additionally, AI systems are only as good as the data they are trained on. Bias in data can lead to biased predictions, which can have serious implications in a library setting.

Therefore, it is crucial to approach the implementation of AI in libraries with a clear understanding of what AI is and what it can and cannot do. It is not a magic solution that will solve all of a library's problems, but rather a tool that, when used correctly, can greatly enhance a library's services.

AI is a rapidly evolving field, and staying abreast of the latest developments can be a daunting task. However, understanding the basics of AI is the first step towards harnessing its potential to enhance library services. It is an exciting time to be involved in the library sector, as we stand on the brink of a new era of innovation and transformation powered by AI.

AI and the Digital Age

As we turn the pages of time, we find ourselves in an era where the digital age is not just a concept, but an integral part of our daily lives. This age, marked by the rapid advancement of technology, has changed the way we live, work, and play. The libraries, the bastions of knowledge, are no exception. They are gradually transforming from their traditional roles as repositories of books to becoming digital information hubs, offering a wide range of services to meet the evolving needs of their patrons.

In the heart of this transformation, we find Artificial Intelligence (AI). It's not an overstatement to say that AI has become the backbone of this digital revolution. Its potential to enhance library services is immense and largely untapped. From automating routine tasks to providing personalized services, AI is redefining the library experience for users and staff alike.

Imagine walking into a library where an AI-powered robot greets you, guides you to the appropriate section, and even recommends books based on your reading history. Or consider an online library platform that uses AI to provide a highly personalized experience, suggesting resources based on your search history, academic needs, and personal interests. These are not futuristic fantasies, but realities made possible by the advent of AI.

AI's role in enhancing library services extends beyond user interaction. It promises to revolutionize the behind-the-scenes operations of libraries as well. Cataloging, a crucial but time-consuming task in libraries, can be streamlined with AI. By using machine learning algorithms, libraries can automate the process of classifying and organizing resources, saving considerable time and effort for the staff. This, in turn, allows them to focus more on improving user services.

AI can also play a significant role in preserving and digitizing historical documents. Many libraries house valuable collections of rare books, manuscripts, and other documents that are deteriorating with time. AI-powered systems can aid in the digitization of these resources, ensuring their preservation for future generations. Moreover, AI can also help in making these digitized resources more accessible by transcribing handwritten texts, translating documents into different languages, and even creating interactive multimedia presentations.

The potential of AI in enhancing library services is not without challenges. Issues related to privacy, data security, and the digital divide are of significant concern. Libraries need to ensure that the use of AI does not compromise the privacy of users or the security of their data. Also, they need to strive to make these AI-enhanced services accessible to all users, regardless of their digital literacy levels.

Moreover, the successful implementation of AI in libraries requires a significant investment in terms of resources and training. Libraries need to invest in the right technology and train their staff to use it effectively. They also need to keep abreast of the latest developments in AI to continually improve their services.

In this rapidly changing digital age, libraries cannot afford to be left behind. AI offers them an opportunity to enhance their services, improve user experience, and stay relevant. By embracing AI, libraries can transform themselves into dynamic, user-centric information hubs catering to the diverse needs of their patrons in this digital age.

Role of AI in Libraries

The tale of artificial intelligence is one that unfolds in unexpected corners, and libraries are no exception. Indeed, the world of literature and information is evolving, and AI is a key player in this transformation. Libraries, once quiet sanctuaries of books and hushed whispers, are now becoming centres of technological innovation. Through the integration of AI, traditional library services are witnessing an unprecedented enhancement, resulting in improved efficiency, accessibility, and user engagement.

Consider the task of sorting and categorizing books. Once a laborious process requiring meticulous attention and countless hours, AI can now streamline these tasks with remarkable precision and speed. Machine learning algorithms, a subset of AI, are capable of analyzing and organizing vast amounts of data. In a library setting, these algorithms can be taught to categorize books based on their content, author, genre, and more, thereby ensuring a more efficient and accurate system of organization.

Similarly, AI has also revolutionized the way libraries handle information retrieval. Gone are the days of sifting through card catalogs or manually searching for a specific book on the shelves. AI-driven search engines and recommendation systems can help users locate the exact book they need, and even suggest related materials based on their search history and preferences. This not only saves time but also enriches the user's experience by exposing them to new literature they might not have discovered otherwise.

But the role of AI in libraries extends beyond mere organization and search capabilities. AI can also assist in preserving and digitizing historical documents. Libraries often house centuries-old manuscripts that are slowly deteriorating with time. AI can help in the digitization of these documents, capturing their content before they are lost forever. Moreover, AI algorithms can analyze these texts, extracting important information and making it accessible to the public. This can greatly aid researchers and historians in their work, opening up new avenues of study and understanding.

Furthermore, AI can enhance the accessibility of library services. For instance, AI-powered chatbots can provide round-the-clock assistance to users, answering queries and guiding them through the library's resources. For individuals with disabilities, AI can be a game-changer. Speech recognition and text-to-speech technologies can make library resources accessible to those with visual impairments, while sign language recognition systems can assist those with hearing impairments.

However, the integration of AI in libraries is not without its challenges. Issues of privacy, data security, and the digital divide are pertinent. Libraries, being public institutions, must ensure that the use of AI respects user privacy and confidentiality. Moreover, they must make AI-driven services accessible to all, regardless of their digital literacy or access to technology.

Nonetheless, the potential benefits of AI in enhancing library services are immense. From improving efficiency and accessibility to preserving historical documents, AI is indeed redefining the library landscape. As we move forward, it is crucial for libraries to adapt and harness the power of AI, all the while maintaining their commitment to inclusivity, privacy, and the promotion of knowledge. In this evolving narrative of libraries and AI, one thing is certain: the story is just beginning.

Future of AI in Libraries

As we turn the pages of technological advancements, the future of artificial intelligence (AI) in libraries is a tale that is yet to be fully written, but the early chapters are already promising. Amidst the whispering pages and the silent corridors of the libraries, AI is transforming the traditional narrative of library services.

Imagine walking into a library where an AI-powered robot greets you by name, having recognized you from your last visit. It asks about your research topic and promptly guides you to the relevant section, suggesting resources and even offering a summary of each. This future is not as far-fetched as it may seem. AI is progressively making its presence felt in libraries, serving as a quiet yet powerful ally in organizing and delivering information.

AI's potential to enhance libraries lies in its ability to sift through vast amounts of data, identify patterns, and provide insightful recommendations. This could revolutionize how libraries manage their collections, facilitating a more efficient system of cataloguing and retrieving books and other resources. Additionally, AI can help libraries to better understand and meet the needs of their users. For instance, by analyzing users' borrowing habits and search queries, AI can provide personalized recommendations, enhancing the user experience.

Moreover, AI could play a pivotal role in preserving and digitizing historical documents. AI tools equipped with machine learning algorithms can transcribe and translate old manuscripts, making them accessible to a wider audience. They can also identify and repair damaged sections in digital images of documents, preserving precious historical information.

However, the transition towards an AI-driven library is not without its challenges. The most significant of these is the ethical concern surrounding data privacy. Libraries have always been trusted institutions where users can seek information freely. The use of AI, which often involves collecting and analyzing user data, could potentially jeopardize this trust. Thus, libraries must ensure that their use of AI respects user privacy and adheres to ethical guidelines.

Training library staff to work with AI tools is another challenge. Not everyone is tech-savvy, and some may even be resistant to change. Therefore, libraries will need to invest in professional development programs to equip their staff with the necessary skills to effectively use AI.

Furthermore, libraries must also consider the financial implications of implementing AI. While AI can undoubtedly bring numerous benefits, it can also be a significant investment.

Libraries must carefully weigh the costs against the potential benefits to ensure that their investment in AI is worthwhile.

As we delve deeper into the story of AI in libraries, we must remember that AI is not a replacement for librarians, but rather a powerful tool that can augment their capabilities. Librarians' expertise in information management and their commitment to serving users' information needs are irreplaceable. AI can help librarians to provide better, more personalized services, but it cannot replicate the human touch that makes libraries such special places.

The future of AI in libraries is a story that is still being written. As we continue to explore the potential of AI, we must remember to balance its benefits with the need to preserve the integrity of libraries as trusted, user-focused institutions. With careful planning and consideration, the integration of AI into libraries can lead to a future where libraries are more efficient, accessible, and responsive to user needs.

Chapter 2: AI for Streamlining Library Operations

Automating Cataloguing

Imagine stepping into a library where every book, every manuscript, every periodical, and every piece of media is perfectly catalogued. A place where finding the desired information no longer involves sifting through stacks of books or scrolling through endless online databases. Instead, you type your request into a search bar, and within seconds, you have a list of materials precisely matching your requirement. This is not a distant dream, but a reality made possible by AI.

The process of cataloguing, a vital task for any library, involves the systematic recording of items in a collection. Traditionally, this process has been manual, requiring substantial time and effort from librarians. However, with the advent of Artificial Intelligence (AI), the landscape of cataloguing is being transformed.

AI has the potential to automate the cataloguing process, making it more efficient and accurate. It can analyze and categorize items based on numerous parameters such as author, title, subject matter, publication date, and more. AI can also recognize patterns and make connections between items that human cataloguers might miss, leading to a more comprehensive and interconnected library catalog.

Moreover, AI can handle vast amounts of data. In large libraries with thousands or even millions of items, manual cataloguing can be a daunting task. However, AI can process these large data sets with relative ease, making the cataloguing process faster and less prone to human error.

One of the ways AI can automate cataloguing is through machine learning, a subset of AI that involves training a computer system to learn and improve from experience. For instance, a machine learning model can be trained to recognize and categorize items based on their features. Over time, the model becomes better at this task, leading to more accurate cataloguing.

Another AI approach to cataloguing involves natural language processing (NLP), which allows a computer system to understand and interpret human language. This can be especially useful for cataloguing items that involve text, such as books or manuscripts. NLP can analyze the text and determine the subject matter, allowing the item to be categorized accordingly.

AI can also enhance the cataloguing process through image recognition. This technology can be used to catalog items that involve visual content, such as photographs or artwork. Image recognition can analyze the visual content and categorize the item based on what it 'sees'.

The benefits of AI in cataloguing extend beyond efficiency and accuracy. By automating the cataloguing process, librarians are freed from this time-consuming task and can focus on other important aspects of their job, such as helping users find and access materials, conducting research, and planning programs and events.

However, the use of AI in cataloguing also presents challenges. For instance, AI systems need to be trained and monitored to ensure they are working correctly. There are also ethical considerations related to the use of AI, such as issues of privacy and bias.

Despite these challenges, the potential benefits of AI in automating cataloguing are significant. With continued advancements in AI technology, the future of library cataloguing looks promising. The day when every item in a library is perfectly catalogued could be closer than we think.

AI for Inventory Management

As we delve deeper into the realm of artificial intelligence, we find ourselves amidst a fascinating intersection of technology and inventory management. For a library, inventory management is not just about keeping track of books and other resources. It is about ensuring that the right resources are available at the right time to meet the needs of library users. Traditional methods of inventory management often involve labor-intensive processes and can be prone to errors. But with artificial intelligence, we are witnessing a transformation that is making inventory management more efficient and effective.

One of the ways AI is enhancing inventory management is through predictive analytics. AI algorithms are capable of analyzing past borrowing patterns, seasonal trends, and other factors to predict future demand for different resources. This allows libraries to maintain an optimal inventory, reducing the risk of overstocking or understocking. Additionally, AI can help libraries identify patterns and trends that may not be immediately apparent to human librarians. For instance, the AI could reveal that certain books or resources tend to be borrowed together, providing valuable insights for decision-making regarding inventory and display arrangements.

Artificial intelligence is also making strides in automating routine inventory tasks. For example, AI-powered robots can be employed to scan the shelves and identify misplaced or missing items. These robots can work around the clock, significantly reducing the time and effort required for inventory management. They can also perform tasks with a high degree of accuracy, reducing the risk of errors that can lead to inventory discrepancies.

Another area where AI is proving beneficial is in the management of digital resources. As libraries continue to expand their digital collections, managing these resources becomes increasingly complex. AI can assist by automatically categorizing and tagging digital resources, making it easier for library users to find what they are looking for. Furthermore, AI can provide personalized recommendations based on a user's browsing and borrowing history, enhancing the user experience.

Artificial intelligence is also helping libraries tackle the challenge of managing returned resources. In the past, librarians had to manually check and sort returned items, a process that could be time-consuming and prone to errors. But now, AI-powered systems can automatically sort and reshelve returned items, significantly reducing the workload for library staff.

AI's ability to learn and improve over time is another significant advantage for inventory management. As AI systems continue to interact with library inventory, they become more accurate in their predictions and recommendations. This continuous learning process ensures that the library's inventory management becomes progressively more efficient and effective.

While AI is revolutionizing inventory management, it is important to remember that it is a tool to assist librarians, not replace them. Human librarians bring a level of understanding and empathy that AI cannot replicate. They can interact with library users, understand their needs, and provide personalized service in a way that AI cannot. Therefore, the ideal scenario is a symbiotic relationship where AI and human librarians work together, each contributing their unique strengths to enhance the overall efficiency and effectiveness of the library's services.

In the rapidly evolving landscape of library services, artificial intelligence is proving to be a valuable ally. By enhancing inventory management, AI is not only improving operational efficiency but also elevating the user experience. As we continue to explore the possibilities of AI, we can look forward to a future where libraries are more responsive, adaptive, and user-friendly.

AI in Book Recommendation

As we delve deeper into the realm of artificial intelligence and its potential applications, let's turn the page to an intriguing aspect - book recommendations. Libraries, once considered a sanctuary for book lovers, are now transforming into tech-savvy spaces. This metamorphosis is not just about digitizing the book collection or offering e-books, but it's about integrating AI to enhance the user experience by providing personalized book recommendations.

AI has the potential to revolutionize the way libraries operate. It can not only automate the routine tasks but also offer personalized services to the users. Among these, the most notable aspect is book recommendation. This is where AI can play a pivotal role, transforming the way readers discover new books.

In the era of information overload, finding a book that aligns with one's interest can be a daunting task. This is where AI steps in, sifting through thousands of titles, analyzing patterns and predicting what a user might like to read next. AI uses machine learning algorithms to analyze a user's reading history and preferences, offering suggestions that are likely to be of interest.

The beauty of AI lies in its ability to learn and adapt. The more a user interacts with the system, the better it gets at understanding their preferences. Over time, the AI's recommendations become more accurate, providing a more personalized and satisfying user experience.

For instance, consider a user who has a penchant for mysteries set in Victorian England. Traditional recommendation systems might suggest other mystery novels or books set in the same era. However, an AI-powered system could dig deeper, recommending books that feature strong female protagonists, based on the user's past reading patterns. This level of detail is only possible with AI's ability to analyze and learn from large amounts of data.

Moreover, AI can also help libraries in managing their collections more efficiently. By analyzing borrowing patterns and popularity of different genres, AI can provide valuable insights into what books to acquire and which ones to retire, ensuring the library's collection remains relevant and appealing.

Furthermore, AI can also bridge the gap between digital and physical libraries. By integrating AI technology with digital platforms, libraries can offer personalized recommendations to users even when they are not physically present in the library. This can increase engagement and encourage more users to take advantage of library services.

Despite the potential benefits, the integration of AI in libraries is not without challenges. Privacy concerns are paramount, as AI systems require access to user data to provide personalized recommendations. Libraries will need to ensure that user data is handled securely and ethically. Additionally, there is the question of digital divide. Not all users may have access to digital platforms or be comfortable using them. Libraries will need to consider these factors and work towards solutions that are inclusive and accessible to all.

AI in book recommendation is an exciting development, offering a new way for readers to discover books and for libraries to engage with their users. It presents an opportunity for libraries to reinvent themselves, moving from a traditional book-lending model to a more dynamic, personalized service. While the path to integration may have its challenges, the potential benefits make it a journey worth undertaking.

AI in Data Analysis

As we delve deeper into the realm of artificial intelligence, we encounter an area where AI has profoundly transformed how we operate: data analysis. Libraries, the longstanding guardians of knowledge, are not exempt from this revolution. In fact, they stand to benefit immensely from the advancements in AI, particularly in improving their services through data analysis.

One might wonder, how does AI fit into the picture of data analysis in libraries? Well, imagine a library as a vast ocean of information, where each book, journal, and digital resource is a unique species of marine life. In this ocean, librarians are the explorers, tasked with navigating the depths, understanding the ecosystem, and guiding patrons to the resources they seek. However, the sheer volume of information can be overwhelming. This is where AI steps in, acting as an advanced navigation system, helping librarians map out the ocean of information, understand its patterns, and deliver a more efficient service.

AI, with its machine learning algorithms, can sift through large volumes of data, analyze patterns, and make predictions. For libraries, this can mean analyzing borrowing patterns, identifying popular topics, predicting future demands, and even suggesting books based on a patron's reading history. Such insights can help libraries optimize their stock, improve their services, and offer a more personalized experience to their patrons.

Moreover, AI can assist in the more complex task of semantic analysis. By 'reading' and understanding the content of books and other resources, AI can categorize and tag them more accurately. This not only enhances the search functionality but also aids in the discovery of new, relevant resources. Imagine a patron looking for resources on climate change. With AI, the library system could not only provide books specifically titled 'climate change' but also suggest resources related to environmental policy, green energy, or biodiversity, thus broadening the patron's research scope.

AI also has a significant role in digital libraries, where the amount of information is even more vast and diverse. Here, AI can help manage and analyze data from different formats - be it text, image, audio, or video. For instance, AI can analyze an audio or video file, transcribe it, and make it searchable, thus enhancing accessibility. Similarly, AI can analyze images, identify objects or text within them, and make them searchable as well. Such capabilities can drastically improve the user experience in digital libraries.

However, the integration of AI into library services is not without its challenges. Issues of privacy, data security, and ethical use of AI are of paramount importance. Libraries, being trusted institutions, must ensure that the use of AI respects user privacy and does not compromise data security. Furthermore, the AI systems must be transparent and explainable, so that librarians understand how a particular suggestion or prediction was made.

As we move forward, the role of AI in data analysis for libraries is set to become even more significant. It presents an opportunity to revolutionize how libraries function, making them more efficient, more responsive to their patrons' needs, and more capable of handling the ever-increasing volume of information. It's an exciting time for libraries, as they harness the power of AI to enhance their services, and in turn, enrich the lives of their patrons.

Chapter 3: AI for Enhancing User Experience

AI-Powered Search Engines

As we delve into the realm of artificial intelligence and its application in library services, it becomes inevitable to discuss the role of AI-Powered Search Engines. These intelligent systems are transforming the ways in which we access and interact with information, effectively revolutionizing library services.

Artificial intelligence, or AI, is the simulation of human intelligence processes by machines, particularly computer systems. When applied to search engines, AI can significantly enhance their efficiency and accuracy. AI-powered search engines use complex algorithms to learn from user behavior and preferences, thereby providing more relevant and personalized search results. This is a significant departure from traditional search engines, which rely on static algorithms and keyword matching.

AI-powered search engines are essentially learning machines. They learn from every search query and every click, constantly refining their algorithms to improve future search results. This learning process is what makes AI-powered search engines more effective and efficient than their traditional counterparts. They can understand the context and intent behind search queries, allowing them to provide more accurate and relevant results.

In the context of library services, AI-powered search engines can dramatically enhance the user experience. They can help users find the information they need more quickly and easily, saving them time and effort. For instance, if a user is searching for books on a specific topic, an AI-powered search engine can provide personalized recommendations based on the user's search history and preferences.

Moreover, AI-powered search engines can help libraries manage their collections more efficiently. They can analyze user behavior and trends to identify popular and underutilized resources. This information can help libraries make informed decisions about acquisitions and deaccessions, ensuring that their collections remain relevant and useful to their users.

AI-powered search engines can also support librarians in their work. They can automate routine tasks such as cataloguing and indexing, freeing up librarians to focus on more complex and high-value tasks. Furthermore, they can provide librarians with valuable insights into user behavior and needs, helping them improve library services and programs.

However, the implementation of AI-powered search engines in library services is not without challenges. It requires significant investment in technology and infrastructure, as well as the development of new skills and competencies among library staff. Privacy and security are also major concerns, as AI-powered search engines collect and analyze large amounts of user data.

Despite these challenges, the potential benefits of AI-powered search engines for library services are immense. They promise to make information access more efficient, personalized, and user-friendly. They can help libraries stay relevant in the digital age, meeting the changing needs and expectations of their users.

As we move forward, it becomes clear that AI-powered search engines are not just a trend, but a fundamental shift in how we access and interact with information. They represent a new era in library services, one that is powered by artificial intelligence. The future of libraries lies not in the stacks, but in the algorithms.

AI in Virtual Assistance

In a world where technology is evolving at a rapid pace, libraries are not being left behind. Artificial Intelligence (AI) has found its place in library services, and one of the most significant ways it's making an impact is through virtual assistance.

Imagine walking into a library and being greeted by a virtual assistant who knows your reading preferences, suggests new books based on your taste, and even assists you in locating the books in the library. This is no longer a figment of imagination but a reality in some technologically advanced libraries. AI, with its capabilities to understand, learn, and predict human behavior, is revolutionizing the way libraries function.

The AI-powered virtual assistant in libraries is akin to a knowledgeable librarian who knows every book in the library and can provide suggestions based on a myriad of factors. The AI analyzes the user's past reading habits, the popularity of books, the latest trends, and even the user's mood to suggest the most suitable books. This not only enhances the user's experience but also saves significant time that the user would otherwise spend searching for books.

Furthermore, the virtual assistant can also manage administrative tasks such as issuing and returning books, sending reminders for due dates, and even handling fines. This automation of administrative tasks liberates the librarians from mundane tasks, allowing them to focus more on enhancing the user experience and other critical tasks.

The AI-powered virtual assistant also has a significant role in facilitating research. The assistant can analyze the vast amount of data available in the library databases and provide the most relevant information to the users. It can even provide insights into the latest research trends and suggest resources that the user might not have considered. This not only saves time for the users but also ensures a more comprehensive and efficient research process.

Moreover, the virtual assistant can also be programmed to assist users with special needs. For instance, it can read out books for visually impaired users or suggest books in Braille. It can also assist users with hearing impairment by providing textual information. This inclusivity provided by AI significantly enhances the library experience for all users.

AI in libraries is not just about enhancing user experience and efficiency. It also plays a crucial role in managing and organizing the vast amount of data that libraries deal with. The AI can analyze the usage data to understand the popularity of books, peak usage times, and other trends. This can help in better management of resources and planning for the future.

While AI in libraries, particularly in the form of virtual assistance, holds immense potential, it also raises certain concerns. The most significant of these is the privacy of user data. As the AI analyzes user behavior and preferences, it is essential to ensure the privacy and security of this data. Libraries, therefore, need to have robust data protection policies in place.

As we move further into the digital age, the role of AI in libraries is set to become even more significant. With its ability to enhance user experience, facilitate research, manage data, and provide inclusivity, AI is truly transforming libraries into technologically advanced, user-friendly spaces. However, it is essential to balance this technological advancement with the need for data privacy and human touch. AI can supplement human librarians but can never replace them. After all, a library is not just about books and technology; it's also about the human connection and the joy of exploring the world of knowledge.

Personalized User Experience with AI

As we delve deeper into the realm of AI, it's crucial to understand how it can be leveraged to personalize the user experience within a library setting. Imagine walking into a library where the environment is tailored to your unique preferences, where the system understands your reading habits, and recommendations are customized to your taste. This is the future that AI promises for library services.

One of the most exciting aspects of AI is its capacity for machine learning. This is the process through which AI systems learn from data and improve over time. In the context of a library, machine learning could be used to analyze a user's reading history and make personalized recommendations. This not only enhances the user's experience but also saves time and effort.

Imagine a scenario where a student is writing a research paper on climate change. The AI system in the library, having analyzed the student's past reading history and understanding their current need, can provide a list of resources - books, articles, documentaries - on that topic. The AI system can also suggest researchers or experts in the field the student might want to reach out to. This level of personalization can greatly enhance the student's research process, making it more efficient and less stressful.

Moreover, AI can also help in creating personalized learning paths. Based on the user's reading history, the AI system can suggest a series of books or resources that can help them understand a subject better. For instance, if a user has been reading beginner level books on data science, the system can suggest intermediate level books or online courses to help them further their understanding. This personalized learning path can help users achieve their learning goals more effectively.

AI can also be used to create a more engaging and interactive user experience. For instance, AI-powered chatbots can provide 24/7 assistance to library users, answering their queries, helping them find resources, or even guiding them through the library. These chatbots can be programmed to understand natural language, making the interaction more human-like and less robotic.

Furthermore, AI can help libraries become more accessible. For users with visual impairments, AI can provide audio descriptions of books or resources. For those who are hard of hearing, AI can provide subtitles or transcripts of audio resources. By making libraries more accessible, AI ensures that everyone, regardless of their abilities, can benefit from the wealth of knowledge that libraries hold.

The potential of AI in enhancing library services and creating a personalized user experience is immense. However, it's also important to approach this with caution. Privacy concerns are paramount when personalizing user experience. Libraries must ensure that they respect user privacy and use data responsibly.

Also, while AI can enhance the user experience, it cannot replace the human touch. The role of librarians remains crucial in guiding, advising, and helping users navigate through the sea of information.

As we move forward, it's clear that AI has a pivotal role to play in transforming library services. By personalizing the user experience, AI can make libraries more efficient, accessible, and engaging, thereby enriching the journey of learning and discovery for all.

AI for User Engagement

As we delve deeper into the universe of artificial intelligence, it becomes evident that AI has the potential to revolutionize library services. One of the most significant aspects of this revolution is the impact on user engagement. Libraries are no longer just repositories of books but vibrant centers of community interaction, learning, and engagement. AI has the potential to enhance this engagement, offering personalized experiences, facilitating discovery, and improving accessibility.

Imagine walking into a library and being greeted by a virtual assistant capable of understanding and responding to your queries. This is not a distant reality but a possibility enabled by AI. Chatbots, powered by AI, can act as virtual librarians, assisting users in finding resources, answering queries, and even recommending books based on past preferences. This personalized interaction can significantly enhance user engagement, making the library experience more interactive and user-friendly.

Furthermore, AI can be instrumental in facilitating discovery. With the sheer volume of resources available in libraries, finding relevant material can sometimes be akin to finding a needle in a haystack. AI can streamline this process, using algorithms to recommend resources based on a user's search history, preferences, and behavior. This not only simplifies the discovery process but also introduces users to new materials they might not have come across otherwise.

AI can also improve library accessibility, making resources available to a wider audience. For instance, AI-powered transcription services can convert audio resources into text, making them accessible to the hearing impaired. Similarly, AI can translate resources into different languages, breaking down language barriers and making resources accessible to non-English speakers. This inclusive approach can significantly boost user engagement, attracting a diverse user base.

Moreover, AI can be used to analyze user behavior and engagement patterns. This data can provide valuable insights, helping libraries understand what works and what doesn't, and adapt their services accordingly. For instance, if data shows that users are more engaged with digital resources than physical books, a library might choose to invest more in expanding its digital collection.

However, while AI offers numerous benefits, it also brings challenges. Issues of privacy and data security are paramount. Libraries need to ensure that they are using AI in a way that respects user privacy and protects data. Additionally, as libraries increasingly rely on AI, they must also ensure that they have the necessary infrastructure and skills to support this technology.

Despite these challenges, the potential of AI to enhance user engagement is undeniable. It can transform libraries from passive repositories of information into dynamic, interactive spaces. It can make libraries more accessible, inclusive, and user-friendly. And most importantly, it can help libraries stay relevant in a digital age, attracting new users and retaining existing ones.

In essence, AI has the potential to redefine user engagement in libraries. And while the journey may be fraught with challenges, the rewards are well worth the effort. As we move forward, it is crucial that libraries not only embrace AI but also actively explore ways to leverage this technology to enhance their services and user engagement.

Chapter 4: AI for Fostering Accessibility

AI in Text to Speech Conversion

As you delve deeper into the world of artificial intelligence and its potential to revolutionize library services, one particular application stands out - the conversion of text to speech. Imagine, if you will, a bustling library in the heart of a city. Students, researchers, and avid readers alike scramble to find the resources they need, often spending countless hours pouring over text-heavy books and documents. Now, picture a scenario where they could simply listen to the information they seek. The integration of AI in text to speech conversion can make this vision a reality.

Artificial intelligence's influence on text to speech technology is profound. It starts with a process known as natural language processing (NLP), a branch of AI that allows computers to understand, interpret, and replicate human language. NLP algorithms can analyze a written text, understand its context and nuances, and convert it into spoken words. This technology can be a game-changer in libraries, enabling a more accessible and inclusive environment for all patrons.

Consider those with visual impairments or dyslexia, for whom reading traditional print materials can be a daunting task. AI-powered text to speech services can provide these individuals with an alternative way to access information, breaking down barriers and promoting inclusivity. Similarly, for individuals whose first language is not English, text to speech services can help them better understand and digest complex texts.

Moreover, the use of AI in text to speech conversion can also enhance the overall user experience in libraries. Many people today are constantly on the move, trying to juggle multiple tasks at once. For such individuals, being able to listen to a book or an article while commuting or doing chores can be incredibly beneficial. It allows them to make efficient use of their time and ensures they don't miss out on valuable information.

From a library management perspective, the integration of AI in text to speech conversion can also lead to operational efficiency. It can reduce the need for physical space, as more materials can be made available digitally. This can result in significant cost savings in terms of storage and maintenance. Furthermore, it can also help libraries broaden their reach, as digital materials powered by text to speech services can be accessed by patrons from anywhere, at any time.

However, the journey towards integrating AI in text to speech conversion in libraries is not without challenges. The quality of the speech output, for instance, is a critical factor. While AI has significantly improved the fluency and naturalness of synthesized speech, there is still room for improvement. Issues related to privacy and data security also need to be addressed, as AI systems often require access to vast amounts of data to function effectively.

In spite of these challenges, the potential benefits of AI in text to speech conversion are too significant to ignore. As we move towards a more digital and inclusive future, libraries must leverage this technology to enhance their services and foster a culture of accessibility and inclusivity. With AI, the possibilities are endless, and the future of library services looks promising.

AI in Visual Assistance

Imagine stepping into a library, a vast repository of knowledge, filled with an overwhelming number of books, journals, and digital resources. As you navigate through the labyrinth of literature, your eyes are your primary guide. But what if your vision isn't perfect? Or worse yet, what if you're visually impaired? This is where Artificial Intelligence, particularly in the form of visual assistance, comes into play.

Artificial Intelligence (AI) has dramatically transformed various sectors, and the library services are no exception. It offers a new dimension of accessibility, particularly for visually impaired individuals, by enhancing the visual assistance features in libraries.

Visual assistance powered by AI can help identify and sort books, read text aloud, and even guide users through the library's physical space. AI-powered visual assistance can transform the library experience for all users, but it's especially revolutionary for those with visual impairments.

Imagine a visually impaired person using an AI-powered app on their smartphone. The app could identify book titles and authors, read out the text, and even guide them to the book's location. The application uses AI to analyze images captured by the phone's camera, identify the text and objects, and convert this information into audio. This way, the user can navigate the library independently, find what they need, and even read it.

But the magic of AI in visual assistance doesn't stop there. AI can also help in sorting and managing books. Libraries can use AI-powered robots to sort books based on their titles, authors, or genres. These robots use AI to recognize the text on the book covers and sort them accordingly. This not only saves time but also reduces the chances of human error.

Moreover, AI can also provide personalized recommendations to the users. Based on the user's reading history, AI can suggest books or authors they might like. This feature can be particularly useful for visually impaired users, as it reduces the time and effort they need to find books that match their interests.

AI in visual assistance can also help in maintaining the library's digital resources. It can categorize and tag digital images, videos, and documents, making them easily searchable. For example, AI can identify the content of a digital image, tag it with relevant keywords, and make it searchable. This way, users can easily find digital resources related to a specific topic or theme.

AI can also help in improving the library's website accessibility. It can analyze the website's design and content and suggest improvements to make it more accessible for visually impaired users. This could include increasing contrast, enlarging text, or adding alt text to images.

AI in visual assistance is not just about making libraries more accessible. It's also about making them more efficient, personalized, and user-friendly. By embracing AI, libraries can provide a better service to all their users, regardless of their visual abilities.

However, implementing AI in visual assistance is not without challenges. It requires significant investment in technology and training. Libraries also need to consider privacy and ethical issues related to the use of AI. Despite these challenges, the benefits of AI in visual assistance are undeniable. It has the potential to revolutionize the library experience, especially for visually impaired users.

In the age of digital transformation, libraries must leverage AI to enhance their services. AI in visual assistance can make libraries more accessible, efficient, and personalized. It's not just a tool for the future; it's a tool for today.

AI for Accessible Content Creation

In the realm of libraries, the creation of content accessible to all is paramount. Here, artificial intelligence has a crucial role to play, making content more inclusive and user-friendly. The vast potential of AI is increasingly being harnessed to create content that can be accessed by people with varying abilities and preferences, thus achieving a more inclusive library environment.

One of the prime examples where AI is making a significant impact is in the field of assistive technology. Text-to-speech and speech-to-text technologies, powered by AI, are helping those with visual impairments or dyslexia to access content that was previously inaccessible. By converting written text into audible speech or vice versa, AI is breaking down barriers and opening up a world of knowledge previously closed to many.

Moreover, AI is making strides in translation services. Libraries often house content in multiple languages, and AI can help make this content accessible to a broader audience. Machine learning algorithms can automatically translate text into different languages, making it easier for non-native speakers to access and understand the content. This not only expands the reach of the library but also fosters a more inclusive and diverse environment.

AI can also facilitate the creation of alternative text descriptions for images, a feature that is particularly beneficial for visually impaired users. By analyzing an image, AI can generate a description that can be read out loud, providing context and understanding for those who cannot see the image. This not only makes content more accessible but also enriches the user experience.

Furthermore, AI can assist in making video content more accessible. Automatic captioning and transcription services can make video content accessible to individuals who are deaf or hard of hearing. AI can automatically generate captions for videos, which can then be read on screen or converted into Braille. This not only makes the content more accessible but also enhances user engagement and comprehension.

AI is not just about making content accessible; it's also about making the process of creating content more efficient. AI can help in content curation, organization, and classification, making it easier for librarians to manage and distribute content. Machine learning algorithms can analyze and categorize content, making it easier to find and access. This can save librarians a significant amount of time and effort, allowing them to focus on other important tasks.

Furthermore, AI can assist in the detection and correction of errors in content. AI algorithms can spot inconsistencies, typos, and grammatical errors, ensuring the content is accurate and of high quality. This not only improves the user experience but also enhances the reputation of the library as a reliable source of information.

The integration of AI in libraries is still in its early stages, but the potential is enormous. As technology continues to advance, we can expect even more innovative and effective ways to make content creation more accessible and efficient. By embracing AI, libraries can ensure they remain relevant and essential in the digital age, providing a service that is inclusive, efficient, and of high quality.

AI in Remote Access to Library Services

As the digital age continues to evolve, libraries are no longer confined within the four walls of a brick-and-mortar building. The Internet has revolutionized the way we access information, and libraries have adapted to this change, offering remote access to their resources. Artificial Intelligence (AI) plays a pivotal role in enhancing these remote library services, making it easier for users to access and utilize library resources from the comfort of their homes or anywhere in the world.

AI has transformed the traditional library into a smart library, where users can search and retrieve information with ease. Search engines powered by AI algorithms can understand the user's search intent and provide more accurate and relevant results. For instance, semantic search engines understand the context of the user's query, providing results that are not just based on keywords but also on the meaning behind those words. This significantly improves the user's experience, making information retrieval more efficient and precise.

AI also plays a significant role in personalizing the user's experience. Through machine learning, AI can analyze a user's search history and behavior, predicting their needs and preferences. This allows the library to recommend resources that are tailored to the user's interests, enhancing their engagement and satisfaction. For instance, if a user frequently accesses resources related to environmental science, the AI system can recommend new books, articles, or research papers on that topic.

AI-powered chatbots are another innovation enhancing remote library services. These virtual assistants can interact with users in real-time, answering their queries and guiding them through the library's resources. They can help users find specific resources, explain how to access e-books or online databases, or even assist in troubleshooting technical issues. This not only improves the user's experience but also reduces the workload of library staff, allowing them to focus on more complex tasks.

In addition to improving user services, AI also aids in managing and organizing the library's resources. AI algorithms can analyze and categorize resources based on various parameters such as subject, author, or publication date. This helps in maintaining an organized and up-to-date digital catalog, making it easier for users to find and access resources.

Moreover, AI can help in predicting trends and patterns in resource usage. By analyzing data such as the frequency of resource access, peak usage times, or popular topics, AI can provide valuable insights for library management. These insights can guide decision-making, helping libraries to optimize their services, allocate resources effectively, and plan for future needs.

AI's role in enhancing remote library services is not limited to these applications. With advancements in technology, AI's potential in this field is vast and continually growing. From voice recognition to predictive analytics, AI technologies are set to revolutionize library services in ways we can only imagine.

However, the integration of AI in remote library services is not without challenges. Issues such as data privacy, algorithmic bias, and the digital divide need to be addressed. Libraries need to ensure that AI technologies are used ethically and inclusively, benefiting all users regardless of their digital literacy skills or access to technology.

Despite these challenges, the benefits of AI in remote library services are undeniable. As libraries continue to adapt to the digital age, AI will play an increasingly important role in enhancing user services, improving resource management, and shaping the future of libraries.

Chapter 5: Practical Examples of AI in Libraries

Case Study: AI in Academic Libraries

Once upon a time, in the heart of a bustling university, there sat an old academic library. For years, it stood as a cornerstone of knowledge, housing countless books, journals, and research documents. But as technology advanced, the library found itself struggling to keep pace with the changing needs of its users.

As students and researchers turned more and more to digital resources, the library's traditional methods of cataloguing and managing its vast collection started to show their age. It was becoming increasingly difficult to navigate the library's resources. The staff, although dedicated and hardworking, were overwhelmed. It was clear that something needed to change.

Enter Artificial Intelligence (AI), a technological marvel that had the potential to revolutionize the library services. With its ability to learn, adapt, and automate, AI offered an innovative solution to the library's growing challenges. The library staff, recognizing the potential of AI, decided to integrate it into their system.

The first step was to implement AI in cataloguing. Traditionally, cataloguing was a laborious task that required manual input from the library staff. But with AI, this process could be automated. Machine learning algorithms were trained to recognize and categorize books based on their titles, authors, and subjects. This not only saved the staff valuable time but also made the library's catalogue more accurate and efficient.

Next, AI was used to enhance the library's search function. The traditional keyword-based search was often ineffective, returning irrelevant results or missing out on key resources. AI, however, could understand the context and nuances of a search query, providing more accurate and relevant results. This made it easier for students and researchers to find the resources they needed.

AI was also used to improve the library's user services. An AI-powered chatbot was introduced to handle routine inquiries, freeing up the staff to focus on more complex tasks. The chatbot was programmed to answer questions about library hours, book availability, and even provide research assistance. It was available 24/7, ensuring that users could get help whenever they needed it.

Furthermore, AI was used to analyze the library's usage data. By tracking which books were borrowed most frequently, which resources were most searched for, and which services were most used, the AI could identify trends and patterns. This information was invaluable in helping the library make informed decisions about its collection and services.

The impact of AI on the academic library was profound. The library's services became more efficient and user-friendly. The staff, relieved of routine tasks, were able to focus on more meaningful work. And the students and researchers found it easier to navigate the library's resources, enhancing their learning and research experience.

This transformation of the academic library is a testament to the power of AI. It shows how AI can be used to enhance library services, making them more efficient, accurate, and user-friendly. As technology continues to evolve, the role of AI in libraries is likely to grow, shaping the future of library services in ways we can only imagine.

And so, the old academic library, with the help of AI, was able to reinvent itself. It became a beacon of modernity in the heart of the university, a testament to the power of technology and innovation in enhancing library services. And in doing so, it ensured that it would continue to serve as a cornerstone of knowledge for many years to come.

Case Study: AI in Public Libraries

Public libraries, the bastions of knowledge and community engagement, are not immune to the sweeping changes brought about by the advent of artificial intelligence (AI). As they continue to evolve, their role in the digital age is expanding to include the use of AI to enhance library services. The story of AI implementation in public libraries is one of innovation, challenge, and opportunity, offering valuable insights for any institution seeking to leverage technology for public service.

Imagine walking into a public library and being greeted not by a human librarian, but by an AI-powered robot. This is not a scene out of a science fiction novel, but a reality at the Longmont Public Library in Colorado. This robot, named Bibli, can answer questions, recommend books, and even host storytime for children. It is a shining example of how AI can be used to augment human services in a library setting.

However, the use of AI in public libraries is not limited to robots. Libraries are also utilizing AI in the form of chatbots for customer service, machine learning algorithms for book recommendations, and data analysis tools for optimizing library operations. For instance, the Los Angeles Public Library uses an AI chatbot to answer common patron queries, freeing up human librarians to tackle more complex issues.

These AI applications are not without their challenges. Privacy concerns are paramount, given that libraries have always been trusted custodians of patron information. The use of AI tools that collect and analyze user data presents potential risks to this trust. Therefore, libraries implementing AI must ensure robust data protection measures are in place.

Another challenge is the digital divide. While AI can certainly enhance library services, not all patrons have the technological literacy to utilize these services effectively. Libraries must therefore play a dual role: introducing AI-powered services while also providing digital literacy training to ensure these services are accessible to all.

Despite these challenges, the potential benefits of AI in public libraries are immense. AI can automate routine tasks, freeing up librarians to focus on more high-value activities such as community outreach and program development. Furthermore, AI tools can provide personalized recommendations to patrons, enhancing their library experience and encouraging increased engagement.

Moreover, AI can help libraries become more data-driven. Through AI-powered data analysis, libraries can gain insights into patron behavior and preferences, enabling them to make more informed decisions about resource allocation, program development, and service offerings.

One of the most exciting prospects is the role of libraries as facilitators of AI education. As public spaces dedicated to learning and information access, libraries are ideally positioned to provide AI education to the community. By offering workshops, resources, and even AI-powered tools for patrons to experiment with, libraries can help demystify AI and empower individuals with the knowledge and skills to navigate the AI-driven world.

The story of AI in public libraries is still being written, with each chapter revealing new possibilities and challenges. From robotic librarians to AI-powered data analysis, the integration of AI into library services is transforming the way libraries operate and serve their communities. As this story unfolds, one thing is clear: the future of public libraries lies at the intersection of human ingenuity and artificial intelligence. For those who hold the library dear, this is a future full of promise.

Case Study: AI in Special Libraries

In the realm of special libraries, where unique collections and specialized services are the norm, the integration of Artificial Intelligence (AI) is transforming the way these institutions function and serve their users. To better understand this evolution, let's delve into a case study that highlights the adoption and impact of AI in special libraries.

The National Library of Medicine (NLM) in the United States offers a compelling example. As one of the world's largest biomedical libraries, the NLM has a vast collection of literature, including books, journals, technical reports, and much more. With the aim of improving access to this extensive collection, the NLM has incorporated AI into its services.

The NLM's AI-powered 'PubMed' search engine is a prime example. This tool uses Natural Language Processing (NLP), a branch of AI that deals with the interaction between computers and human language, to enhance the search experience. It understands user queries in a more human-like manner, allowing for more accurate and relevant search results. This has resulted in improved accessibility to the library's vast biomedical literature, enabling researchers to find the information they need more efficiently and effectively.

Moreover, the NLM has also implemented an AI-based chatbot to assist users. This chatbot can answer common queries, guide users through website navigation, and provide information about library services and resources. This AI tool not only reduces the workload of library staff but also ensures that users get immediate assistance, enhancing user satisfaction.

The NLM's use of AI extends to its document digitization process as well. The library uses Optical Character Recognition (OCR), an AI technology that recognizes text within a digital image, to digitize its vast collection of printed materials. This technology has significantly sped up the process of making these resources available online, thereby increasing the reach of the library's unique collection.

The impact of AI on the NLM's services is clear: improved search capabilities, enhanced user engagement, and increased accessibility to resources. However, it's also important to note that the integration of AI did not happen overnight. It required careful planning, investment, and training of staff to understand and effectively use these AI tools.

The NLM's experience provides valuable insights for other special libraries considering AI implementation. It highlights the potential of AI to enhance library services and the importance of strategic planning and investment in AI integration. However, it also underscores the need for ongoing training and support to ensure that library staff can effectively use these tools and adapt to changing technologies.

The use of AI in special libraries, as exemplified by the NLM, is not just about adopting new technologies; it's about leveraging these technologies to better serve library users. It's about using AI to enhance accessibility, improve user engagement, and ultimately, provide better library services.

This case study underscores the transformative potential of AI in special libraries. As AI technologies continue to evolve, they offer exciting possibilities for enhancing library services, from improving search capabilities to digitizing collections and beyond. However, the successful integration of AI requires strategic planning, investment, and ongoing training and support. It's a journey worth embarking on, given the potential rewards: improved services, satisfied users, and a more efficient, effective library.

Case Study: AI in Digital Libraries

In the realm of libraries, digital or otherwise, the potential of Artificial Intelligence (AI) is immense. Let's delve into the heart of a case study that exemplifies this potential: the adoption of AI in digital libraries.

The story begins with a typical digital library, brimming with thousands of resources, from ebooks and journals to multimedia content. The challenge, as with any library, was to facilitate easy access to these resources. The library's conventional search and categorization tools were no longer adequate in the face of the growing volume and diversity of materials. The solution? AI.

The first step in the library's AI journey was the implementation of an AI-powered search engine. This wasn't just any search engine, but one equipped with Natural Language Processing (NLP) capabilities. NLP allowed the search engine to understand and process user queries as a human would, providing more accurate and relevant results. For instance, if a user queried "Shakespearean tragedies," the AI could understand that the user was looking for tragedies written by Shakespeare, rather than a generic search for the words 'Shakespeare' and 'tragedies'. This was a significant improvement over traditional keyword-based search engines.

Next, the library adopted an AI-based recommendation system. This system leveraged Machine Learning (ML) algorithms to analyze user behavior and preferences and suggest resources that the user might find interesting. The recommendation system functioned much like the ones we see on ecommerce or streaming platforms, making the library experience more personalized and engaging.

The library's AI transformation didn't stop there. It also incorporated AI into its cataloging and metadata generation processes. An AI tool was developed to automatically generate metadata for new resources, including information about the resource's content, author, publication date, and more. This not only saved librarians a significant amount of time but also improved the consistency and accuracy of the library's metadata.

The AI's role also extended to handling user inquiries. The library introduced an AI-powered chatbot to answer common questions from users, such as queries about library hours, resource availability, and borrowing policies. The chatbot was programmed to learn from each interaction, gradually improving its ability to provide accurate and helpful responses.

The impact of these AI implementations was profound. Users reported a significant improvement in their ability to find and access resources. The library saw an increase in user engagement, and librarians found that they had more time to focus on more complex tasks, as the AI took care of routine tasks.

The AI's benefits extended beyond the library's users and staff. The library's parent institution also reaped benefits, as the improved accessibility and usability of the library's resources supported research and learning activities across the institution. Moreover, the library's successful AI implementation served as a model for other libraries and institutions, inspiring them to explore the potential of AI in their own contexts.

In this case study, we've seen how AI can transform a digital library, improving both user experience and operational efficiency. It's a compelling example of how AI can enhance library services, bringing benefits to users, librarians, and institutions alike. While this is just one case study, the possibilities for AI in libraries are vast and exciting. From AI-powered search and recommendation systems to automated cataloging and customer service, AI is poised to revolutionize the way we think about and interact with libraries.

Chapter 6: Strategies for Implementing AI in Libraries

Understanding the Library's Needs

In the quiet hum of the library, nestled between rows of books and illuminated under the soft glow of reading lamps, the librarian stands as the gatekeeper of knowledge. For years, this role has evolved, adapting to the changing needs of those who frequent these hallowed halls. Today, as we step into a world increasingly powered by artificial intelligence (AI), the library is poised for yet another transformation. To fully leverage AI and enhance their services, libraries must first understand their needs.

To begin with, the library is more than just a repository of books. It is a hub for community engagement, a platform for learning, and a sanctuary for those in search of knowledge or solace. Libraries today cater to a diverse demographic, each with unique needs and expectations. Understanding these needs is the first step towards enhancing library services.

The most fundamental need is access to information. In an era where information is abundant, the challenge is not in its availability but in its discovery. With thousands of books, periodicals, and digital resources, finding the right information can be akin to finding a needle in a haystack. AI can help streamline this process by providing smart search and recommendation systems, making it easier for users to find what they need.

Next, consider the need for personalization. With the advent of digital technologies, users are increasingly expecting personalized experiences. Libraries need to move away from a one-size-fits-all approach and adopt a more user-centric model. AI can enable this by analyzing user behavior and preferences to provide personalized recommendations and services.

Furthermore, libraries need to address the demand for digital literacy. As technology permeates every aspect of our lives, digital literacy has become a critical skill. Libraries, as centers of learning, have a responsibility to educate their users about these new technologies. AI can be used to create interactive learning platforms, making the process of learning digital skills more engaging and effective.

Then, there is the need for accessibility. Libraries must be accessible to people of all abilities, ensuring that everyone can benefit from their services. AI can play a significant role here, from voice recognition systems that help visually impaired users to predictive text and sign language recognition for those with hearing or speech impairments.

Moreover, libraries must also consider their internal needs. Managing a library involves a multitude of tasks, from cataloging books to managing user accounts. AI can automate many of these tasks, freeing up librarians to focus on more strategic initiatives.

Finally, libraries need to ensure their sustainability. In a world where budgets are tight, libraries need to prove their value and ensure their continued relevance. AI can provide insights into user behavior and preferences, helping libraries to make data-driven decisions and demonstrate their impact.

In the end, understanding the library's needs is not just about identifying the challenges they face. It's about recognizing the opportunities these challenges present. It's about envisioning a future where libraries are not just repositories of books, but vibrant, inclusive, and technologically advanced centers of learning. And most importantly, it's about acknowledging that AI, with all its potential, is not the end but a means to achieve this future.

Choosing the Right AI Tools

As we delve further into the subject, it's crucial to understand that not all AI tools are created equal. The vast landscape of artificial intelligence technologies can be overwhelming, and it's important to choose the right tool that best fits the specific needs of your library. The ideal AI tool can help libraries offer enhanced services, streamline operations, and provide an enriched user experience.

You may consider several factors when selecting the right AI tool for your library. First and foremost, the tool must be relevant to your library's needs. For example, if your library is looking to automate its cataloging process, an AI tool specializing in natural language processing and machine learning would be highly effective.

Understand the needs of your library and its patrons. An AI tool that is capable of adapting and learning from user behavior can drastically improve the overall user experience. AI tools that use machine learning algorithms can analyze user data to provide customized recommendations, enhancing the user's journey through the library's resources.

The selected AI tool should be user-friendly and easy to navigate. Remember, the ultimate goal is to enhance the library experience for your patrons. A tool that is overly complex or not intuitive can deter users from taking full advantage of the library's resources. Therefore, consider tools that have clear instructions, user-friendly interfaces, and provide excellent customer support.

The budget is another significant factor when choosing an AI tool. The cost of AI tools can vary greatly. Some tools might offer sophisticated features but come with a hefty price tag. On the other hand, more affordable options might provide fewer features but still meet your library's needs. It's important to strike a balance between cost and functionality.

Next, consider the reliability and accuracy of the AI tool. Libraries deal with vast amounts of data and information that need to be managed accurately. A tool that often makes errors or fails to deliver the expected results can cause more harm than good. Look for tools that have a proven track record of reliability and accuracy.

Aside from these factors, it's also worth considering the scalability of the AI tool. As your library grows and evolves, so too will its needs and challenges. The AI tool you choose should be able to scale and evolve with your library. This means it should have the capacity to handle increased data volumes, more complex tasks, and new functionalities as required.

Moreover, consider the security features of the AI tool. Libraries handle a lot of sensitive data, and it's crucial that this information is handled with utmost care. The AI tool you choose should come with robust security features to ensure the safety and privacy of your library's data.

Lastly, consider the tool's integration capabilities. The AI tool should easily integrate with your existing library management system. This will ensure a seamless transition and allow you to fully leverage the capabilities of the AI tool.

In the vast realm of AI tools, finding the perfect fit for your library can seem like a daunting task. However, by keeping these considerations in mind, you can navigate the landscape with confidence, ensuring your library reaps the maximum benefits from AI technology. Remember, the right tool can significantly enhance the library services you offer, transforming your library into a dynamic, user-centric, and highly efficient entity.

Training Staff for AI Integration

As dawn breaks on the era of artificial intelligence, libraries stand on the precipice of a revolution. The potential benefits are immense - improved efficiency, increased accessibility, and the ability to offer more personalized services to patrons. However, the successful integration of AI into library services is contingent upon one critical factor: the staff.

Imagine a library where AI systems have been intricately woven into the fabric of everyday operations. The staff, however, are unable to use these systems effectively. The result? A library that is less efficient and less accessible than before. This scenario underscores the importance of training library staff for AI integration.

To begin with, the training should aim to demystify AI. For many, the term 'artificial intelligence' conjures up images of humanoid robots or complex mathematical equations. While these perceptions are not entirely unfounded, they can be intimidating and may deter staff from fully embracing AI. Therefore, the first step in training should be to explain what AI is - and what it isn't. Staff should understand that AI is a tool, like any other, designed to help them provide better services.

Next, the training should focus on the practical aspects of using AI. Staff should be taught how to operate the AI systems that have been integrated into the library's operations. This includes not only the technical aspects, such as how to enter commands or troubleshoot common issues, but also the conceptual aspects, such as when to use AI and when to rely on human judgment. Practical, hands-on training will give staff the confidence they need to use AI effectively.

Moreover, staff should be educated about the ethical implications of using AI. As with any technology, AI can be misused, and it is vital that staff understand the responsibilities that come with its use. This includes respecting patrons' privacy, ensuring fairness in the services provided, and being transparent about the use of AI.

A successful training program will also acknowledge the diverse range of skills and experiences among library staff. Some staff members may already have a basic understanding of AI, while others may be starting from scratch. Some may be tech-savvy, while others may be less comfortable with technology. A one-size-fits-all approach will not work. Instead, the training should be tailored to meet the needs of each staff member, ensuring that everyone is equipped to contribute to the library's AI journey.

Furthermore, training should not be a one-time event. As AI continues to evolve, so too should the training. Regular refresher courses and updates on new developments will ensure that staff are always at the cutting edge of AI use in libraries.

In essence, training is more than just a box to be checked off in the process of integrating AI into library services. It is a critical investment in the library's most valuable resource: its people. By empowering staff with the knowledge and skills to use AI effectively, libraries can unlock the full potential of this revolutionary technology. The result is a library that is not just surviving in the age of AI, but thriving.

Thus, the integration of AI into library services is akin to learning a new language. It is not enough to simply acquire new vocabulary (the AI systems); one must also understand the grammar (the principles and ethics of AI use), and practice speaking (using AI in everyday operations). And just as with language learning, the key to success is good teaching. For libraries, this means investing in training their staff for AI integration.

Evaluating the Success of AI Implementation

As we delve deeper into the intricacies of AI integration in our libraries, the question of measuring the success of such an endeavor inevitably arises. It's a critical stage that must not be overlooked, for it provides valuable feedback and insights that can guide future decisions and strategies. So, how do we assess the effectiveness of AI implementation in enhancing library services?

We must first acknowledge that success in this context is multifaceted. It's not just about the technological accomplishment but also about the positive impact on library services, user satisfaction, and the overall improvement in library operations. Therefore, to gauge success, we must set clear, measurable objectives before the AI implementation process begins.

One of the primary indicators of a successful AI integration is its effect on library operations. The AI system should streamline processes, reduce manual work, and increase overall efficiency. For instance, AI-driven chatbots should effectively handle user inquiries, leading to a decrease in the workload of library staff. A reduction in the time taken to perform routine tasks or a notable increase in operational efficiency are good indicators of success.

Next, we must consider user satisfaction. AI is being implemented to enhance user experience, so their feedback is invaluable. Surveys and feedback forms can be used to determine if the users find the AI enhancements helpful and easy to use. Are they satisfied with the AI-driven services? Do they find the AI-powered search and recommendation systems accurate and useful? A high level of user satisfaction signifies that the AI implementation is successful.

Thirdly, we must look at the impact of AI on the library's key performance indicators (KPIs). These could include increased user engagement, higher borrowing rates, or increased usage of online resources. A significant improvement in these metrics post-AI implementation is a strong sign of success.

The AI system's adaptability and learning capability is another essential factor. A successful AI system continuously learns and improves from user interactions. Over time, it should provide more accurate responses and predictions. This continuous learning and improvement indicate that the AI system is functioning as it should.

The cost-effectiveness of the AI system is also a crucial measure. The AI integration should bring about operational savings in the long run, whether through reduced manpower costs or increased efficiency. While initial implementation costs might be high, the system should eventually pay for itself through the benefits brought about.

It is also worth considering the library staff's feedback. They are the ones who will work closely with the AI system, and their opinions on its functionality and effectiveness are crucial. Have they found the system helpful, or has it made their work more complicated? Staff feedback can provide insights into any issues that might not be apparent from the user feedback or operational data.

In essence, evaluating the success of AI implementation in libraries requires a comprehensive look at various factors. It involves considering the operational efficiency, user and staff satisfaction, improvement in KPIs, the system's learning capability, and cost-effectiveness. This holistic approach ensures that the AI system is not just technologically sound but also effective in enhancing library services and the overall user experience.

Chapter 7: Ethical Considerations in AI Implementation

Privacy and AI

In the hushed silence of a library, enveloped by the comforting scent of old books and the soft rustle of turning pages, one may not immediately think of cutting-edge artificial intelligence (AI). Yet, it is precisely this quiet sanctuary of knowledge where AI is making a marked impact, enhancing the delivery of library services in ways that were once the stuff of science fiction. However, with this innovative leap into the future, an important question arises - how does the introduction of AI impact privacy in the library?

The kaleidoscope of AI applications in libraries is vast and continually expanding. From automated book sorting systems to intelligent recommendation engines, AI is revolutionizing the way libraries function. But this brings with it a paradoxical challenge. While AI can undoubtedly enhance the efficiency and personalization of library services, it also requires access to vast amounts of data – data that often includes sensitive information about library users. In the wrong hands, or even just mishandled, this information could pose serious privacy risks.

Consider, for instance, an AI-powered library system that tracks a user's reading habits to recommend books. While this seems like a convenient feature, it also means the system is gathering, analyzing, and storing data about the user's preferences. In a world where data is a precious commodity, who has access to this information? How is it stored and protected? And, how can it be used or misused? These are all critical questions that must be addressed when implementing AI in libraries.

Moreover, as AI grows more sophisticated, so does its ability to collect and analyze data. Advanced algorithms can infer personal details about users from seemingly innocuous data points. For example, a user's reading list could reveal their political leanings, religious beliefs, health concerns, or other sensitive information. This kind of data privacy concern is not unique to libraries but applies to all sectors where AI is deployed.

So, how can libraries harness the power of AI while also preserving the privacy of their users? One solution is through robust data protection measures. Libraries must ensure that any data collected for AI applications is securely stored and protected from unauthorized access. Additionally, users should be informed about the data being collected and how it will be used, giving them the option to opt-out if they wish.

Another solution lies in the design of the AI system itself. AI developers can incorporate privacy-preserving technologies, such as differential privacy, which allows the system to learn from data without revealing specific details about individuals. Such techniques ensure that AI can still provide personalized recommendations without compromising user privacy.

AI's integration into library services is an exciting development that promises to revolutionize the library experience. However, it is essential to navigate this new frontier with care, balancing the benefits of AI with the fundamental right to privacy. By implementing robust data protection measures and incorporating privacy-preserving technologies into AI design, libraries can offer enhanced services without sacrificing user privacy.

The quiet sanctuary of the library is evolving, and with thoughtful consideration of privacy issues, it can remain a trusted space for knowledge and discovery in the AI era. The tale of AI in libraries is still being written, and it is up to us to ensure that it is a story of progress, innovation, and respect for our privacy.

Bias and AI

In the dawn of the digital age, libraries are evolving beyond their traditional role as repositories of knowledge. They are becoming dynamic hubs for learning, research, and community engagement. Amidst this transformation, artificial intelligence (AI) emerges as a powerful tool to enhance library services. However, as we weave AI into the fabric of library operations, we must also grapple with an inherent challenge—bias in AI.

Bias in AI is not about machines developing a mind of their own. Instead, it reflects the biases present in the data used to train these AI systems. Think of AI as a mirror that reflects the world around it, including its prejudices and stereotypes. If the data used to train AI is biased, the AI system will inevitably perpetuate this bias. This is particularly concerning in a library setting, where fairness, equity, and inclusivity are cornerstones of service.

Consider, for instance, a library using AI to suggest books to patrons. If the training data includes a disproportionate number of books by male authors or on Western topics, the AI system may end up recommending these books more often. This not only narrows the diversity of literature presented to patrons but also reinforces existing biases.

Furthermore, bias in AI can also manifest in how it interacts with users. AI chatbots, for instance, are becoming increasingly common in libraries, helping patrons with queries and book recommendations. However, if these chatbots are trained on data that lacks representation from diverse linguistic and cultural backgrounds, they may struggle to understand and respond to queries from patrons who do not communicate in 'standard' English. This could inadvertently exclude certain patrons from accessing the full range of library services.

So, how can libraries navigate this challenge? The key lies in acknowledging the potential for bias and taking proactive steps to mitigate it. This starts with diversifying the data used to train AI systems. Libraries should strive to include a broad range of books, authors, and topics in their training data. Similarly, for AI chatbots, libraries should include data from diverse linguistic and cultural backgrounds.

Libraries can also leverage AI to actively combat bias. For example, AI can be used to analyze the library's collection and identify gaps in representation. This could include underrepresented authors, topics, or demographics. Libraries can then use this information to diversify their collections and ensure they are providing equitable access to knowledge.

Moreover, libraries should cultivate transparency around their use of AI. They should communicate to patrons how AI is used, what data it is trained on, and how it impacts the services they receive. This fosters trust and allows patrons to make informed choices about their interaction with AI.

In the quest to leverage AI for enhancing library services, it is critical to remember that AI is not neutral. It is a tool that, like any other, bears the imprint of its creators and the data it is fed. By acknowledging and addressing bias in AI, libraries can ensure that they continue to uphold their values of fairness, equity, and inclusivity in the digital age.

Transparency and AI

In the vast realm of artificial intelligence, there exists an often-overlooked facet known as transparency. This is a crucial aspect that plays a vital role in the successful implementation of AI in enhancing library services. To comprehend this concept better, imagine a library patron asking the AI-powered library assistant a question. The AI assistant responds, but the patron is left wondering, "How did it know that?" This is where transparency comes into play.

Transparency in AI refers to the explainability and understandability of the decision-making process of AI systems. In the context of libraries, transparency enables patrons and librarians to understand how the AI-powered library assistant works, how it processes information, and how it arrives at a particular answer or solution. This understanding fosters trust in the system and encourages users to interact more confidently with it.

A transparent AI system in library services would provide clear, understandable explanations for its actions. For instance, if a patron asks for book recommendations based on a particular genre, the AI system could explain that it is suggesting certain books because they are highly rated by other readers who enjoy the same genre. This provides the patron with an understanding of how the AI system operates and instills confidence in its recommendations.

However, achieving transparency in AI is not an easy task. AI systems are often complex and multi-layered, making their decision-making processes difficult to understand. This complexity is further compounded when AI systems are trained using machine learning algorithms, where they learn and improve from experience without being explicitly programmed. In such cases, the AI system's decision-making process can become a 'black box,' opaque and incomprehensible to users.

To overcome this challenge, libraries can adopt various strategies. One approach is the use of explainable AI (XAI) models, which are designed to provide clear and understandable explanations for their decisions. Another strategy is to involve librarians in the development and training of AI systems. As information professionals, librarians have a deep understanding of their patrons' needs and can help ensure that the AI system is designed to meet those needs in a transparent and user-friendly manner.

Moreover, libraries can also undertake efforts to educate patrons about AI. They can organize workshops or seminars to explain how AI works and how it is used in the library. This not only enhances transparency but also empowers patrons, enabling them to interact more effectively with the AI-powered library services.

However, it's important to remember that transparency should not compromise the privacy and security of users. Libraries should ensure that their AI systems respect user privacy and handle personal data securely. They should also be transparent about their data handling practices, informing users about what data is collected, why it is collected, and how it is used.

In essence, transparency is a two-way street. On one hand, it requires AI systems to be clear and understandable in their operations. On the other hand, it requires libraries to be open and forthcoming about their use of AI. When these two aspects of transparency are achieved, libraries can successfully harness the power of AI to enhance their services, providing a more engaging and enriching experience for their patrons.

Accountability and AI

As we delve deeper into the realm of artificial intelligence (AI) and its potential to revolutionize library services, we must also consider the implications of accountability. To whom should the AI be accountable, and how can we ensure its actions are transparent and ethical? These are critical questions that need to be addressed as libraries increasingly incorporate AI into their systems and services.

Accountability, in the context of AI, involves holding the AI system and its developers responsible for the decisions it makes and the actions it takes. As we have seen in previous chapters, AI has the potential to significantly enhance library services, from automating routine tasks to personalizing user experiences. However, with this potential comes a responsibility to ensure that the AI is acting in a manner that is fair, unbiased, and respectful of user privacy.

One of the key challenges in ensuring accountability in AI systems is the so-called 'black box' problem. This refers to the fact that many AI algorithms, particularly those based on deep learning, are opaque and difficult to interpret. This lack of transparency can make it hard to understand why an AI system made a particular decision or took a particular action. This is a significant concern in the context of library services, where decisions made by AI could impact the information that users are provided with or the services they are able to access.

To overcome this challenge, there is a growing emphasis on developing 'explainable AI' (XAI). XAI is a subfield of AI that focuses on creating systems that can provide clear, understandable explanations for their decisions and actions. This can help to ensure accountability by making it possible to understand and question the AI's actions. In the context of libraries, this could involve the AI providing explanations for why it recommended a particular book or resource, or why it prioritized certain search results over others.

Another key aspect of accountability in AI is ensuring that the system respects user privacy. Libraries have a long-standing commitment to protecting user privacy, and this must extend to the use of AI. This can be a complex issue, as many AI systems rely on large amounts of data to function effectively. However, there are strategies that can be used to balance the need for data with the need to respect user privacy. For example, libraries could use 'differential privacy', a technique that allows for the use of large datasets while ensuring that the information about individual users is kept private.

In addition, libraries need to ensure that their use of AI is ethically sound. This involves considering the potential impacts of AI on users and society more broadly, and taking steps to mitigate any negative effects. For example, libraries could implement policies to ensure that their AI systems do not reinforce or perpetuate existing biases, and that they promote diversity and inclusivity.

The use of AI in libraries presents exciting opportunities to enhance services and improve user experiences. However, it is crucial that libraries approach the use of AI with a sense of responsibility and accountability. By focusing on transparency, privacy, and ethics, libraries can ensure that their use of AI is not only effective, but also respectful of their users and their values.

Chapter 8: Challenges in AI Implementation

Technological Challenges

As we delve deeper into the realm of artificial intelligence (AI) and its potential impact on library services, we are faced with a variety of technological hurdles. These challenges, while daunting, provide opportunities for growth and innovation. They are the stepping stones on our path to fully integrating AI into the library ecosystem, reshaping the way we provide services to our users.

The first challenge lies in the development and implementation of AI technology itself. It's no secret that AI is a complex field, with numerous sub-disciplines and specializations. It requires a high level of expertise to create AI systems that are capable of performing tasks with the same level of accuracy and efficiency as a human. Libraries, as public institutions, are often constrained by budgets and resources, making it difficult to invest in the high-cost development of AI systems.

Moreover, even if libraries could afford to develop their own AI systems, they would still face the challenge of integrating these systems into their existing infrastructure. Libraries have been around for centuries, and many still rely on legacy systems and outdated technology. These systems were not designed with AI in mind, and modifying them to accommodate AI technology can be a monumental task.

Data privacy and security is another significant concern. Libraries are custodians of a vast amount of sensitive user information, ranging from personal details to borrowing histories. The use of AI technology, which often involves the collection and processing of large amounts of data, raises serious questions about how to protect this information and ensure it is not misused.

Furthermore, there is the challenge of making AI technology accessible and understandable to library users. AI is a highly technical field, and it can be intimidating for those who are not familiar with it. Libraries will need to find ways to demystify AI and educate their users about how it is being used to enhance services, while also addressing any fears or misconceptions that people may have about the technology.

Finally, there is the issue of bias in AI. AI systems are only as good as the data they are trained on. If this data is biased in any way, the AI system will also be biased. This is a particularly pressing concern for libraries, which are committed to providing fair and equal access to information for all users.

Despite these challenges, the potential benefits of AI for library services are too significant to ignore. AI has the potential to revolutionize the way libraries operate, making them more efficient, more user-friendly, and more capable of meeting the needs of their users. But to realize these benefits, libraries will need to navigate the technological challenges that come with AI. This will require a combination of technical expertise, strategic planning, user education, and a commitment to ethical principles.

The journey towards AI-enhanced library services will not be easy. But with careful planning and a clear vision, libraries can overcome the technological challenges and usher in a new era of innovation and service excellence.

Financial Challenges

As the sun rises on a new era of technology, libraries across the globe face a monumental task - to integrate Artificial Intelligence (AI) into their services. However, it's not a path paved with gold. On the contrary, one of the most significant hurdles in this endeavor is the financial aspect.

The cost of implementing AI in libraries is substantial. It's not just about purchasing the technology; it's also about maintaining it. The recurring costs for updates, maintenance, and potential repairs can quickly add up, posing a considerable challenge for budget-restricted libraries. And then, there's the cost of training. Staff needs to learn how to use and manage this new technology effectively, which requires both time and money.

Moreover, the financial burden doesn't end with the implementation phase. The ongoing operation of these AI systems also demands a substantial financial commitment. Libraries must allocate funds for regular updates and security measures to keep the technology current and safe. This ongoing financial commitment can be a significant drain on resources over time.

A further financial challenge lies in the unpredictable nature of technology. The rapid pace of tech evolution means that what is cutting-edge today may be obsolete tomorrow. Consequently, libraries may find themselves in a constant cycle of investment to keep up with advances in AI. This unpredictability makes budget planning a challenge and can lead to financial instability.

Despite these challenges, it's essential to remember that the benefits of AI in libraries are potentially transformative. AI can automate repetitive tasks, freeing up staff for more complex and engaging work. It can also improve user experiences through personalized recommendations and better search functionality. These benefits, however, come at a price, and libraries must carefully consider their budgets before diving into the world of AI.

Another financial challenge is the potential for increased inequality among libraries. Not all libraries have the same financial resources, and those with smaller budgets may struggle to implement AI. This could lead to a digital divide, where wealthier libraries offer superior services due to their access to AI technology.

In the face of these financial challenges, libraries must be creative and resourceful. They might consider seeking external funding sources such as grants, donations, or partnerships with tech companies. They could also explore cost-sharing models with other libraries or institutions. It's crucial that libraries do not let financial challenges deter them from exploring AI. Instead, they should view them as obstacles to overcome on the path to improved services and user experiences.

As the narrative of AI in libraries unfolds, it's clear that financial challenges are a significant part of the story. However, with careful planning, innovative thinking, and a commitment to equitable service, libraries can navigate these challenges and embrace the opportunities that AI presents. Without a doubt, the journey to integrate AI into library services is a challenging one, fraught with financial hurdles. Yet, it is also a journey filled with promise and potential, making it a story worth telling.

Legal Challenges

As we delve deeper into the world of artificial intelligence and its application in library services, one cannot overlook the maze of legal intricacies that accompany it. Like a double-edged sword, AI brings about a wealth of opportunities as well as a host of legal challenges.

Imagine a scenario where an AI-powered system misinterprets a user's request, resulting in the disclosure of sensitive information. Who would be held accountable? Would it be the library that implemented the AI system or the AI service provider? These are just a few of the many legal conundrums that libraries using AI may face.

Laws pertaining to data privacy are paramount in the digital age. Libraries, as stewards of information, must ensure that the AI systems they employ comply with these laws. AI systems often require large amounts of data to function effectively. This data may include user information such as search history, reading preferences, and personal details. If mishandled, this could lead to significant breaches of privacy. Libraries must therefore ensure that any AI system they use respects user privacy and complies with all relevant data protection laws.

Intellectual property rights are another legal challenge that libraries using AI must contend with. AI systems, particularly those involved in content creation, can inadvertently infringe upon copyrighted material. For instance, an AI system might suggest books or articles to a user based on their reading history, potentially violating copyright laws. Libraries must ensure that their AI systems are designed to respect intellectual property rights and that they have measures in place to prevent any potential infringements.

Liability is another significant legal challenge. If an AI system makes a mistake, who is responsible? Is it the library that implemented the system, the AI service provider, or the user who interacted with the system? The answer to this question is not always clear, and it can vary depending on the specific circumstances of each case. Libraries must therefore have a clear understanding of their legal responsibilities when using AI and ensure that they have appropriate liability protections in place.

The use of AI also raises ethical considerations, which, while not strictly legal issues, can have legal implications. For instance, an AI system might make recommendations based on a user's race, gender, or religion, potentially leading to discrimination. Libraries must ensure that their AI systems are designed to avoid such biases and that they adhere to ethical guidelines.

In the face of these legal challenges, libraries must be proactive. They should seek legal counsel to understand the potential legal implications of using AI and to develop strategies to mitigate these risks. They should also work closely with their AI service providers to ensure that the systems they use are designed to comply with all relevant laws and regulations.

AI holds great promise for enhancing library services, but it also brings with it a host of legal challenges. By understanding these challenges and taking steps to address them, libraries can harness the power of AI while ensuring that they remain within the bounds of the law.

Organizational Challenges

The seamless integration of Artificial Intelligence (AI) into library services is not without its hurdles. The first key challenge is the need for a paradigm shift in organizational culture. Libraries, traditionally seen as the guardians of knowledge, now have to transform into facilitators of knowledge creation. This change involves adopting new technologies like AI and involves a steep learning curve for the staff. It requires a change in mindset from being mere custodians of books to becoming technologically savvy knowledge workers.

The second challenge lies in the training and development of staff. The adoption of AI in library services is not just about installing software or hardware; it requires the staff to understand and utilize these technologies efficiently. This demands a significant investment in staff training. The staff must be trained not only in using AI but also in understanding how AI can enhance the services they provide. This could involve learning new skills, such as data analysis or programming, which could be challenging for some.

The third challenge is the fear and resistance to change. The introduction of AI might be met with fear, skepticism, and resistance from the staff. They might be apprehensive about the potential job losses due to automation or the complexity of the technology. This resistance can slow down the adoption process or even derail it completely. It is essential to address these fears and concerns, highlight the benefits of AI, and assure the staff that their roles are not being replaced but rather enhanced.

The fourth hurdle is the financial implications. The adoption of AI involves a considerable initial investment in terms of purchasing the technology, training the staff, and maintaining the system. Libraries, especially public ones, often operate on limited budgets, making it challenging to secure the necessary funds. Additionally, there are ongoing costs such as software updates, system maintenance, and further training.

The fifth challenge is data privacy and security. Libraries hold vast amounts of sensitive data about their users. With the use of AI, this data could be potentially exposed, leading to privacy concerns. Libraries must ensure they have robust data protection measures in place to maintain the trust of their users.

The sixth challenge is the ethical considerations. AI systems learn from the data they are fed, and if this data is biased, the AI system will also be biased, leading to unfair outcomes. Libraries must ensure that the AI systems they use are transparent, fair, and accountable.

Despite these challenges, the potential benefits of AI in enhancing library services are immense. It can revolutionize the way libraries operate, making them more efficient, user-friendly, and valuable to their communities. However, it is crucial to navigate these challenges carefully, keeping in mind the unique needs and constraints of each library, to ensure successful adoption of AI.

The integration of AI into library services is not a straightforward process. It involves overcoming various organizational challenges, such as changing the organizational culture, training and developing the staff, managing resistance to change, securing funding, ensuring data privacy and security, and addressing ethical considerations. However, with careful planning, these challenges can be overcome, paving the way for libraries to harness the power of AI to enhance their services.

Chapter 9: AI and Library Staff: A New Working Relationship

AI as a Tool, Not a Threat

In the grand tapestry of human knowledge, libraries have always been the vibrant threads weaving together stories, ideas, and discoveries. As the custodians of this tapestry, librarians have traditionally relied on their skills and tools to organize and share this knowledge. Today, Artificial Intelligence (AI) is emerging as a powerful tool enabling librarians to enhance their services, making the library experience more interactive, personalized, and efficient.

Many may view AI with a sense of trepidation, considering it as a threat to job security and personal privacy. Yet, rather than being a looming menace, AI can be a beneficial ally in the library sector. AI isn't here to replace librarians but to augment their abilities, enabling them to provide superior services to library users.

AI can help librarians in various ways. For instance, it can automate routine tasks, freeing up librarians' time to engage in more complex and human-centric activities. Imagine a library where AI systems handle time-consuming tasks such as cataloging new acquisitions or managing lending and returns. Librarians could then focus more on curating exhibitions, organizing community events, or providing personalized research assistance.

AI can also provide better user experiences. With AI, it's possible to create personalized reading recommendations based on users' reading history and preferences, much like how Amazon or Netflix recommends products or movies. This could transform the library experience, making it more engaging and satisfying for users.

Furthermore, AI can help libraries become more accessible. AI-powered services like speech recognition and text-to-speech can make library resources available to people with visual impairments or reading difficulties. In this way, libraries can leverage AI to uphold their mission of providing universal access to knowledge.

AI can also support libraries in preserving and digitizing their collections. AI technologies like Optical Character Recognition (OCR) and machine learning can help in digitizing printed materials, making them searchable and accessible online. Moreover, AI can assist in preserving rare and fragile materials by identifying signs of deterioration and suggesting appropriate preservation measures.

However, harnessing the power of AI in libraries is not without challenges. Issues related to data privacy, algorithmic bias, and digital divide need to be addressed. Libraries, being trusted institutions in society, have a responsibility to ensure that AI is used ethically and equitably.

Libraries need to adopt a proactive approach in dealing with these challenges. They should advocate for transparency in AI algorithms, ensuring that AI systems are fair and unbiased. They should also strive to protect users' data privacy and educate users about their digital rights. Furthermore, libraries should work towards bridging the digital divide by providing access to AI-powered services for all, regardless of their socio-economic status.

Moreover, librarians need to equip themselves with the necessary skills to work with AI. They should understand how AI works and how it can be applied in a library context. This doesn't mean that all librarians should become AI experts. Instead, they should be 'AI-informed' – aware of AI's potential and limitations, and able to make informed decisions about its use in their libraries.

The advent of AI in libraries presents exciting opportunities as well as daunting challenges. But if libraries can harness AI as a tool, not a threat, they can enhance their services, enrich the library experience, and ensure their relevance in the digital age. In the grand tapestry of human knowledge, AI could become the needle that helps librarians weave new patterns of accessibility, personalization, and efficiency.

Upskilling Library Staff for AI

In the realm of library services, the advent of Artificial Intelligence (AI) has necessitated a paradigm shift in the skills required of library staff. This wave of change has presented a unique opportunity for library personnel to expand their repertoire of skills, evolving from traditional roles to becoming adept at harnessing the power of AI to enhance library services.

As the cobwebs of outdated methodologies are dusted off, library staff are being thrust into the world of AI, a realm that may seem daunting and alien. However, with the right training, the transition can be a smooth and empowering journey. The challenge lies in transforming library staff from passive users of technology to active manipulators and creators of AI solutions.

This transformation requires an investment in training programs that are designed to impart the necessary skills required to navigate the AI landscape. The goal is not to create a team of AI experts, but rather to equip library staff with a basic understanding of AI and its applications in the library setting. This includes knowledge of AI tools and systems, data analytics, machine learning, and automation.

Training should also focus on cultivating a mindset of innovation. Library staff, armed with AI tools, should be encouraged to identify areas within their work that could benefit from AI applications. This proactive approach to problem-solving will foster a culture of innovation and continuous improvement, which are key to staying relevant in an increasingly digital world.

Some might argue that the upskilling of library staff for AI is a tall order, particularly for those who are not tech-savvy. However, the beauty of AI lies in its ability to be tailored to suit varying levels of technical expertise. Many AI tools are designed to be user-friendly, reducing the barriers to entry. Furthermore, the proliferation of online learning platforms has made it easier than ever to acquire new skills from the comfort of one's desk.

Training library staff for AI is not merely about teaching them to use new tools. It is about inspiring them to embrace the possibilities that AI offers. It is about shifting their mindset from one of fear and apprehension to one of curiosity and excitement. It is about empowering them to leverage AI to improve their work processes, enhance library services, and ultimately, better serve their patrons.

In the grand scheme of things, upskilling library staff for AI is not just about keeping up with the times. It is about future-proofing libraries. As AI continues to permeate various aspects of life, libraries that fail to adapt risk becoming obsolete. On the other hand, libraries that successfully integrate AI into their operations will not only survive but thrive in the era of digital transformation.

The introduction of AI in libraries is a change that is as inevitable as it is transformative. As such, the upskilling of library staff for AI is not just a necessity but an opportunity. An opportunity to enhance library services, to improve staff efficiency, and to redefine the role of libraries in the digital age.

In the narrative of AI and libraries, library staff are the protagonists. Their ability to adapt, learn and innovate will determine the success of AI integration in libraries. Therefore, investing in their training is not just a wise move, but a critical one. It is an investment in the future of libraries, a future that is as exciting as it is promising.

AI and Job Transformation in Libraries

Amidst the rustling of pages and the quiet murmur of studious minds at work, the library of the future is being born. Artificial Intelligence is not just knocking on the door; it is already inside, reshaping the way libraries operate and transforming the job landscape within its hallowed halls.

Artificial Intelligence, or AI, is not a new concept, but its application in the library setting is a relatively recent development. It has been steadily gaining momentum, driven by the need for efficiency, accuracy, and the ability to handle vast amounts of data. AI's impact is not only felt in how library services are delivered but also in the transformation of jobs within the library.

A key area where AI is making a significant impact is in cataloging and classification. These tasks, traditionally performed by librarians, involve painstakingly categorizing and tagging each book or resource. With AI, these tasks can now be automated, which not only speeds up the process but also reduces the risk of human error. This shift enables librarians to focus more on strategic tasks such as planning, policy-making, and community engagement.

Similarly, AI is also transforming the role of reference librarians. These librarians traditionally help patrons find the information they need, a role that requires extensive knowledge of the library's collections. However, with AI-powered search engines and virtual assistants, patrons can now find what they are looking for with a simple voice command or a few keystrokes. This doesn't mean that the role of reference librarians is becoming obsolete. Instead, it is evolving. They are now becoming information consultants, advising patrons on how to navigate the digital world, evaluate the reliability of sources, and understand complex information.

Moreover, AI is opening new job roles within the library. With the incorporation of AI technologies, there is a growing need for AI specialists who can manage and maintain these systems. This includes data scientists, AI ethics experts, and user experience designers. These roles require a blend of technical skills and library knowledge, creating exciting new career paths for library professionals.

While these changes may seem daunting, they also present opportunities for librarians to enhance their skills and adapt to the evolving library landscape. Librarians are no longer just the keepers of books; they are becoming information specialists, digital navigators, and AI experts. They are at the forefront of this digital revolution, guiding patrons through the maze of information and technology.

However, this transformation also brings challenges. There is a need for adequate training and education to equip librarians with the necessary skills to handle these new roles. Libraries must also grapple with ethical issues surrounding the use of AI, including privacy, bias, and transparency.

In the heart of this transformation, one thing remains constant: the library's role as a hub of knowledge and learning. With AI, libraries are not just surviving; they are thriving, providing better services, reaching more people, and opening new avenues of knowledge exploration. The transformation brought about by AI does not diminish the importance of libraries; instead, it amplifies it.

Artificial Intelligence is not the end of the library as we know it but rather a new chapter. It is a tool that, when used wisely, can enhance the library's services, enrich the job roles within it, and ultimately, better serve the community. As we turn the pages of this new chapter, we see the library of the future - a place where AI and human ingenuity coexist, each enhancing the other, each essential in the pursuit of knowledge.

Creating a Collaborative Environment with AI

As we delve deeper into the heart of our discussion, let's shift our focus towards the role of AI in fostering a cooperative environment in libraries. The traditional image of libraries as quiet, solitary spaces is gradually being replaced by a more dynamic and interactive model, thanks to AI's influence.

In today's digital age, libraries are not just repositories of books but are evolving into vibrant community hubs, encouraging collaboration and engagement. AI technology, with its vast capabilities, is instrumental in facilitating this transition. AI-powered tools and applications are being used to create a more inclusive, accessible, and engaging environment in libraries.

Consider the use of AI chatbots as an example. These AI-powered digital assistants are progressively being adopted by libraries worldwide to provide immediate, round-the-clock support to users. They can answer queries, assist with book searches, and even recommend resources based on user preferences, thereby fostering a more interactive and helpful environment. By handling routine queries, these chatbots free up time for library staff to engage more actively with users and provide personalized support.

Furthermore, AI-powered recommendation systems are revolutionizing the way users discover resources in libraries. These systems analyze users' reading habits, preferences, and past searches to suggest books, articles, and other resources. Such personalized recommendations not only enhance user experience but also promote collaboration as users are likely to discuss and share these resources with others.

AI also plays a crucial role in making libraries more inclusive and accessible. For instance, AI-powered speech recognition and language translation tools can help overcome language barriers, enabling users from diverse linguistic backgrounds to access and engage with library resources. Similarly, AI applications like text-to-speech converters can make library resources accessible to visually impaired users.

Moreover, AI can also facilitate collaborative learning in libraries. AI-powered virtual reality (VR) and augmented reality (AR) tools can be used to create interactive learning experiences, promoting collaboration and engagement among users. For example, a group of students can use VR headsets to explore a historical event or scientific concept together, turning the library into a collaborative learning hub.

However, while AI offers immense potential for creating a collaborative environment, it's essential to approach its implementation thoughtfully. Libraries must ensure that the technology is used ethically and responsibly, respecting users' privacy and data security. It's also crucial to provide adequate training to library staff to use and manage AI tools effectively.

Moreover, it's important to remember that AI is not a substitute for human interaction but a tool to enhance it. Libraries should strive to strike a balance between technology and human touch, leveraging AI to facilitate collaboration and engagement while maintaining the warmth and personal connection that make libraries special.

Therefore, AI is not just a tool for enhancing library services but a catalyst for transforming libraries into collaborative, inclusive, and engaging community hubs. By embracing AI, libraries can evolve with the times, meeting the changing needs and expectations of users, while preserving their core values and purpose.

Chapter 10: The Role of AI in Library Programming and Outreach

AI in Library Workshops and Seminars

As you delve deeper into the pages of this book, you will find that artificial intelligence (AI) is not just a buzzword but a transformative force that is reshaping the way libraries function. This chapter specifically explores how AI is revolutionizing library workshops and seminars, making them more efficient, engaging, and personalized.

Libraries have always been the bedrock of learning and information dissemination. However, the advent of AI has expanded their roles, enabling them to offer more than just books. Today, libraries are leveraging AI to facilitate workshops and seminars that cater to the evolving needs of patrons. They are utilizing AI-powered tools to analyze data and predict user behavior, thus developing workshops and seminars that address the specific interests and learning styles of their users.

For instance, AI-driven analytics can help librarians identify popular topics among their user base. Based on the data, they can organize workshops and seminars that align with the users' interests. This not only increases user engagement but also ensures the relevance of the library's offerings.

Moreover, AI can be instrumental in personalizing the learning experience during these events. Libraries can use AI algorithms to tailor content delivery based on individual learning patterns. For instance, if a user learns better through visuals, the AI system can present information in a more graphical or video format during the seminar or workshop. This level of personalization can significantly enhance the learning experience and outcomes.

AI is also enabling libraries to streamline the logistical aspects of organizing workshops and seminars. For instance, AI can assist in scheduling these events at a time that maximizes attendance. It can analyze historical data to identify the days and times when users are most likely to be available. Similarly, AI can predict the resources required for a seminar or workshop based on past trends, thereby aiding in efficient resource allocation.

Libraries are also using AI to improve user engagement during workshops and seminars. For example, AI-powered chatbots can facilitate real-time interaction, answering queries, and providing additional resources. This not only enhances the learning experience but also frees up the librarians to focus on more complex tasks.

Furthermore, libraries can use AI to evaluate the effectiveness of their workshops and seminars. AI tools can analyze user feedback and participation levels to assess the success of these events. The insights gained can then be used to refine future workshops and seminars, making them more effective and user-centric.

However, while AI holds immense potential, it's essential for libraries to use it responsibly. Libraries must ensure the privacy and security of user data while deploying AI. They should also strive to make AI-based services accessible to all users, irrespective of their tech-savviness.

Thus, AI is not just a tool for libraries; it's a partner that can help them redefine their role in the digital age. By leveraging AI, libraries can transform their workshops and seminars into dynamic, personalized, and impactful learning experiences. The possibilities are endless, and as you turn the pages of this book, you will discover how AI is shaping the future of libraries, one workshop, and seminar at a time.

AI in Community Engagement

In the realm of library services, the role of artificial intelligence (AI) has been evolving rapidly, especially in the arena of community engagement. Libraries, as community centers, have traditionally been spaces that foster interaction, knowledge sharing, and collaboration. Today, with the advent of AI, the dynamics of community engagement are transforming, making libraries more interactive, efficient, and user-friendly.

AI facilitates personalized experiences for library users by understanding their interests and preferences. Imagine walking into a library where an AI-powered system recognizes you, knows your reading preferences, and recommends books suited to your taste. It could even suggest related community events, workshops, or discussion groups that might interest you. This level of personalization can significantly enhance user engagement and make libraries more appealing to the community.

Furthermore, AI can help libraries in organizing community events. From scheduling to sending reminders, managing registrations, and gathering feedback, AI can handle multiple administrative tasks, freeing up library staff for more critical roles. For instance, AI chatbots can answer user queries about upcoming events, their timings, venue, or any changes in schedule. This not only makes the process more efficient but also ensures that community members stay well-informed and engaged.

AI can also play a pivotal role in making libraries more inclusive. AI-powered assistive technologies can help visually impaired or differently-abled individuals access library resources with ease. For example, AI-based text-to-speech and speech-to-text systems can enable visually impaired individuals to enjoy books or participate in community discussions. Similarly, AI-powered sign language interpretation systems can help hearing-impaired individuals engage with library resources and events.

The use of AI in libraries is not just limited to enhancing user experiences and inclusivity. AI can also help librarians understand their communities better. By analyzing data on user behaviors, interests, and engagement levels, AI can provide valuable insights into community needs and preferences. These insights can guide librarians in curating resources, planning events, and designing services that resonate with their community.

Moreover, AI can foster a culture of learning and innovation within the community. Libraries can host workshops and discussions on AI, encouraging community members to learn about this technology and explore its applications. This not only enhances community engagement but also promotes digital literacy and lifelong learning.

However, the integration of AI in libraries also raises certain challenges. Concerns about data privacy, algorithmic bias, and digital divide need to be addressed. Libraries need to ensure that AI systems respect user privacy, provide unbiased recommendations, and are accessible to all community members. This requires careful planning, transparent policies, and continuous monitoring.

Libraries have always been at the forefront of adopting new technologies to serve their communities better. With AI, they have an opportunity to redefine community engagement, making it more personalized, inclusive, and insightful. By leveraging AI, libraries can continue to be vibrant community centers in the digital age, fostering a culture of knowledge sharing, innovation, and lifelong learning.

While the journey of integrating AI in libraries may be challenging, the potential benefits for community engagement are immense. With a user-centric approach, ethical considerations, and a commitment to lifelong learning, libraries can harness the power of AI to enhance community engagement and transform library services in the digital age.

AI in Library Marketing and Promotion

As we delve deeper into the realms of artificial intelligence (AI) and its potential applications in library services, we find that its scope extends far beyond simply improving operational efficiency or enhancing user experience. AI has the potential to revolutionize the way libraries market and promote their services, creating new, exciting opportunities for engagement and outreach.

Libraries have always been centers of learning and knowledge, but in the digital age, they face increasing competition from online resources. This is where AI can play a pivotal role. By harnessing the power of AI, libraries can not only compete but also stand out in the digital landscape.

Let's start with personalized marketing. AI can analyze user behavior, interests, and preferences to create highly targeted promotional content. This means that each user gets information about the library services most relevant to them, increasing the likelihood of engagement. Imagine a user who frequently borrows books on photography. An AI system can identify this interest and send them updates about new arrivals in the photography section, photography workshops, or any related events happening in the library. This kind of personalized marketing can significantly improve user engagement and satisfaction.

AI can also be used to create interactive promotional content. Chatbots, for example, can be used to interact with users, answer their queries, and promote library services in a conversational manner. This can be particularly useful for new users who may not be familiar with all the services the library offers. The chatbot can guide them, suggest services based on their interests, and even help them navigate the library.

The power of AI in library marketing and promotion also extends to social media. Libraries can use AI algorithms to analyze social media trends and user behavior, helping them create content that resonates with their audience. AI can also help libraries identify the best time to post content to maximize engagement and reach.

Furthermore, AI can automate routine tasks in marketing and promotion. For instance, AI tools can automatically send out newsletters or updates, schedule social media posts, or even respond to simple queries on the library's website. This not only saves time but also ensures a consistent, timely communication with the users.

AI can also play a role in analyzing the effectiveness of marketing and promotional campaigns. AI algorithms can analyze data on user engagement, feedback, and other metrics to provide insights on what works and what doesn't. This can help libraries improve their strategies and make more informed decisions.

However, the use of AI in library marketing and promotion is not without challenges. Libraries need to ensure that the use of AI respects user privacy and data security. They also need to invest in training staff to use AI tools effectively. Moreover, as AI technologies evolve, libraries need to keep up with the latest developments and adapt their strategies accordingly.

The integration of AI in library marketing and promotion is not an overnight process. It requires careful planning, investment, and a willingness to embrace new technologies. But the potential benefits - increased user engagement, improved efficiency, and a stronger presence in the digital landscape - make it a worthwhile endeavor.

As we move forward in the digital age, AI will continue to shape and redefine the way libraries operate. And in the realm of marketing and promotion, it promises to open up new, exciting avenues for libraries to connect with their users and promote their services in innovative ways. Thus, the future of library marketing and promotion looks bright, and AI is set to play a central role in it.

AI in Library Partnerships and Collaborations

As we delve deeper into the realm of artificial intelligence and its impact on library services, it becomes crucial to explore the role of partnerships and collaborations. The synergy of AI and libraries becomes richer and more potent when different entities come together, bringing their unique perspectives and expertise to the table.

Consider the scenario of a public library system partnering with a tech company specializing in AI. The tech company, with its cutting-edge AI tools, can help the library automate and streamline various tasks, such as cataloging, sorting, and shelving books. The library, in turn, can provide the tech company with valuable insights about user behavior and needs, which can be used to refine and improve the AI tools. This kind of collaboration can lead to the development of more effective and user-friendly AI tools for libraries.

Another form of collaboration involves libraries partnering with educational institutions. Universities and research organizations often have vast resources and expertise in AI and related fields. By partnering with these institutions, libraries can tap into this knowledge and use it to enhance their services. For example, a university's computer science department might collaborate with a library to develop an AI-powered search engine that can understand and respond to complex queries, making it easier for users to find the information they need.

Moreover, collaborations between libraries themselves can also be beneficial. Large library networks, such as the Library of Congress in the United States or the British Library in the UK, can share their experiences and best practices regarding the use of AI. Smaller libraries can learn from these big players and implement similar AI solutions in their own contexts.

These collaborations can also lead to the creation of shared AI resources. For instance, libraries could pool their resources to develop a shared AI tool that can be used by all participating libraries. This would not only save costs but also ensure a consistent user experience across different libraries.

In addition to these forms of collaboration, libraries can also engage with their users to better understand their needs and preferences. AI tools can help libraries gather and analyze user data, but it's also important to have direct conversations with users. By involving users in the development and refinement of AI tools, libraries can ensure that these tools are truly meeting the needs of their users.

Another important aspect of collaboration is the ethical use of AI. Libraries have a responsibility to ensure that the AI tools they use respect user privacy and do not perpetuate biases or discrimination. By collaborating with experts in ethics and law, libraries can ensure that their AI tools are not only effective but also ethically sound.

The possibilities for partnerships and collaborations in the realm of AI and libraries are vast and varied. From tech companies and educational institutions to other libraries and users, there are many potential partners that can help libraries harness the power of AI. Through these collaborations, libraries can enhance their services, provide a better user experience, and fulfill their mission of providing access to information for all.

Chapter 11: Evaluating the Impact of AI on Library Services

Measuring User Satisfaction

As we delve deeper into the realm of Artificial Intelligence (AI) for enhancing library services, it's essential to address a key component that determines the success of any service-oriented endeavor - user satisfaction. It serves as a crucial gauge of the effectiveness of the AI tools implemented and the overall performance of the library services.

In the traditional library setup, gauging user satisfaction was relatively straightforward, involving techniques like surveys, feedback forms, and face-to-face interactions. However, with the integration of AI, the user-library interaction landscape has vastly altered, necessitating the need for novel methods to measure user satisfaction.

AI has the potential to revolutionize the way we perceive user satisfaction. It can provide real-time data about user behavior, needs, and preferences. It can track and analyze user interactions with the system and provide insights that were previously inaccessible. For instance, an AI-powered library system can track which books are most frequently borrowed or which sections of the library are most visited. It can also monitor online user behavior, such as which online resources are most accessed or the average time a user spends on the library website.

However, the richness of data offered by AI also brings forth the challenge of effectively interpreting and utilizing it. It's not enough to merely collect data; one must be able to analyze it in a way that leads to actionable insights. This is where AI proves invaluable, with its ability to process vast amounts of data and identify patterns that can help enhance user satisfaction.

One method of measuring user satisfaction in an AI-enhanced library is through sentiment analysis. This AI technique analyses user feedback, comments, and reviews to gauge the overall sentiment towards the library services. It can identify whether the users are generally satisfied or dissatisfied and pinpoint specific areas of concern or appreciation.

Additionally, an AI system can use predictive analytics to anticipate user needs and preferences. For example, it can recommend books based on a user's borrowing history or suggest resources related to their search history. By proactively addressing user needs, the library can significantly enhance user satisfaction.

AI can also facilitate user engagement, another critical aspect of user satisfaction. For instance, a chatbot can engage users, answer their queries, and guide them through the library services. It can provide 24/7 assistance and ensure that user queries are promptly addressed, thereby enhancing user satisfaction.

However, it's important to note that while AI provides valuable tools for measuring user satisfaction, it doesn't eliminate the need for traditional feedback mechanisms. Surveys and personal interactions still hold value in understanding user needs and preferences. They provide a qualitative aspect to the largely quantitative data provided by AI.

In essence, measuring user satisfaction in an AI-enhanced library involves a blend of traditional feedback mechanisms and AI-powered tools. The goal is to create a synergistic system where AI and human efforts complement each other, leading to a comprehensive understanding of user satisfaction.

As we continue to explore the potential of AI in enhancing library services, user satisfaction remains at the forefront. It's the users that ultimately determine the success of any service, and AI provides an effective means of understanding and addressing their needs. By effectively measuring user satisfaction, libraries can continuously improve their services and ensure that they remain relevant and valuable in the digital age.

Assessing Efficiency Gains

Delving into the world of artificial intelligence (AI) and the possibilities it presents for the modern library, one cannot help but marvel at the potential for efficiency gains. The technological revolution that AI brings to the table is not just about shiny new tools or impressive displays of automation. It's about fundamentally transforming the way libraries operate, making them more effective, more responsive, and more attuned to the needs of their patrons.

When we talk about efficiency in the context of libraries, we're talking about a variety of factors. We're talking about the speed at which services are delivered, the accuracy of information retrieval, the ease of use for patrons, and the ability of library staff to manage resources and tasks. All these elements together contribute to the overall efficiency of library operations.

AI has the potential to significantly improve all these aspects. Let's take the task of cataloging, for instance. Traditionally, this has been a laborious process, requiring meticulous attention to detail and a significant investment of time. With AI, however, libraries can automate this process, using machine learning algorithms to classify and catalog resources. Not only does this save time, but it also reduces the likelihood of human error, ensuring more accurate cataloging.

Similarly, AI can transform the way libraries handle information retrieval. With natural language processing and machine learning, AI can understand and respond to user queries in a more intuitive and accurate manner. This means that patrons can find what they're looking for more quickly and easily, without having to navigate complex databases or rely on library staff.

But the benefits of AI aren't just about speed and accuracy. They're also about personalization. With AI, libraries can tailor their services to the individual needs and preferences of their patrons. For instance, AI can analyze user behavior to recommend resources that are relevant to their interests. This not only enhances the user experience but also helps libraries to utilize their resources more effectively.

In terms of resource management, AI offers significant advantages as well. With predictive analytics, for instance, libraries can forecast demand for different resources, enabling them to manage their collections more effectively. They can also use AI to monitor resource usage and identify patterns, helping them to optimize their services and operations.

Of course, the use of AI in libraries also brings challenges. There are issues of data privacy and security to consider, as well as the need for staff training and the potential for job displacement. However, with careful planning and implementation, these challenges can be managed.

In essence, AI offers a powerful tool for enhancing library services. By automating tasks, improving accuracy, personalizing services, and optimizing resource management, AI can help libraries to become more efficient and effective. The benefits are clear, and the potential is immense. The challenge for libraries now is to harness this potential and navigate the path to AI integration with care and foresight.

In this era of rapid technological change, libraries have a unique opportunity to redefine their role and value. By leveraging AI, they can provide a more efficient, personalized, and responsive service, meeting the evolving needs of their patrons and securing their place in the digital age.

Evaluating the Impact on Staff

As the sun began to set, the library staff gathered in the grand reading room, a place that had witnessed countless discussions and debates over the years. The topic of the evening was the integration of AI into their beloved sanctuary of knowledge.

The air was filled with a blend of anticipation and trepidation. The staff knew that this technology would bring changes, some of which they could predict, while others remained unknown.

The Library Director, a woman of advanced years but with a spirit that danced with curiosity, started the meeting. She began by acknowledging the fears and uncertainties that were palpable in the room. She understood that the staff was worried about job security, the learning curve associated with new technology, and the potential loss of human touch in their services. However, she also emphasized the potential benefits that AI could bring, such as improved efficiency, enhanced user experience, and the opportunity for staff to engage in more complex, creative tasks.

Over the next few weeks, the library staff underwent training to understand and use the new AI systems. They learned how AI could automate routine tasks like sorting and shelving books, answering basic queries, and managing membership records. The staff found that with these tasks taken care of by AI, they had more time to engage with visitors, plan events, and conduct research. They also found that AI could help them provide personalized recommendations to readers, enhancing the user experience.

However, the transition was not without challenges. Some staff members struggled with the new technology. They missed the familiar rhythm of their old tasks and found the AI systems impersonal and intimidating. Others worried about their role in the library. Would they become redundant in a world where machines could do their job more efficiently?

The Library Director reassured them that while AI might change the nature of their work, it could not replace the human touch that they brought to their roles. She reminded them that libraries were not just about books and information but also about human connection and community building. These were areas where AI could not compete with humans.

As the staff grew more comfortable with the AI systems, they began to see the benefits. They found that the systems could handle repetitive tasks with speed and accuracy, freeing them to focus on more important tasks. They also discovered that AI could provide them with insights into user behavior, helping them tailor their services to better meet the needs of the library's users.

Over time, the staff's initial apprehension gave way to acceptance and even enthusiasm. They saw how AI was not a threat but a tool that could help them provide better service to their community. They realized that while AI might change some aspects of their work, it could not replace the passion, creativity, and human connection that they brought to their roles.

As the months passed, the library staff found that AI had not only enhanced their services but also enriched their roles. They had learned new skills, embraced new challenges, and found new ways to serve their community. And in the process, they had become not just librarians, but pioneers in a new era of library service.

The sun had long since set when the staff left the grand reading room that day. As they stepped out into the cool night, they carried with them not just a new understanding of AI, but also a renewed sense of their role and value in the library.

Estimating the Return on Investment

As the pages of our story turn, we delve deeper into the realm of artificial intelligence (AI) and how it significantly impacts library services. In this riveting part of our tale, we scrutinize the economical aspect of implementing AI technologies, particularly in estimating the return on investment (ROI).

Imagine a library, an institution traditionally associated with tranquility and timelessness, as the setting for a dramatic shift in operational efficiency and service enhancement. This transformation is brought about by AI, but it requires a considerable investment. However, like any good investment, it promises substantial returns. The question then arises: how do we measure the ROI?

The answer lies in understanding the key elements that constitute the ROI. Primarily, these are the costs associated with AI implementation and the benefits that arise from it. AI implementation costs include not only the acquisition of the technology itself but also the training of staff to use it effectively. The benefits, on the other hand, are measured in terms of the improved efficiency and quality of library services.

Consider the example of an AI-powered library cataloging system. The initial investment might be substantial, including the cost of the software, hardware, and training. However, once implemented, the AI system can catalog books far more quickly and accurately than human librarians can. This increase in efficiency reduces the time and resources spent on cataloging, translating to significant cost savings in the long run.

The story doesn't end there. The benefits of AI in libraries extend beyond mere cost savings. AI can enhance user experience by providing personalized recommendations, based on their reading history and preferences. This can increase user satisfaction and engagement, leading to higher usage rates, more checkouts, and ultimately, increased library revenues.

Moreover, AI can help libraries expand their services in innovative ways. For instance, AI-powered chatbots can provide round-the-clock assistance to users, answering their queries and helping them navigate the library's resources. This not only improves the quality of service but also frees up librarians' time to focus on more complex tasks.

While these benefits contribute to a positive ROI, quantifying them might be challenging. After all, how do you put a price tag on user satisfaction or the value of a librarian's time? To tackle this, libraries can use metrics such as user surveys to measure satisfaction levels, or time-motion studies to determine the time saved by librarians. They can also compare their usage rates and revenues before and after AI implementation to gauge the impact.

In the grand scheme of things, the ROI of AI in libraries is not just about numbers. It's about enhancing the library's role as a hub of knowledge and learning, empowering librarians to do their jobs better, and enriching the user experience. It's about transforming libraries into dynamic, responsive institutions that are ready to meet the demands of the 21st century.

As we close this chapter, remember that the ROI of AI in libraries is a tale of investment and return, of cost and benefit. It's a story that each library will write in its unique way, depending on its resources, needs, and vision. But one thing is clear: the potential rewards of AI are immense, and for libraries willing to make the investment, the return could be a game-changer.

Chapter 12: Future Trends in AI and Library Services

Predictive Analysis and Libraries

As the dawn of artificial intelligence (AI) casts its light on various industries, the world of library services is not left in the shadows. The potential of AI in transforming and enhancing library services is enormous, with predictive analysis emerging as one of the most promising areas of application.

Predictive analysis is a branch of advanced analytics that uses both new and historical data to forecast activity, behavior, and trends. It involves many techniques from data mining, statistics, modeling, machine learning, and AI to analyze current data and make predictions about the future. In the context of libraries, predictive analysis can significantly enhance library services by enabling librarians to anticipate future trends, user needs, and the usage of library resources.

One of the most significant benefits of predictive analysis in library services is in collection development and management. Libraries have limited resources and must make informed decisions about which books, journals, and other materials to acquire. Predictive analysis can help libraries make these decisions by forecasting which materials will be most in demand in the future, based on factors such as current usage patterns, popular trends, and the academic calendar.

Moreover, predictive analysis can also help libraries improve their user services. By analyzing user behavior and preferences, libraries can predict what services and resources users will need and when they will need them. For instance, a library might predict that demand for study spaces will increase during exam periods and adjust their opening hours or reserve additional spaces accordingly. Similarly, by analyzing borrowing patterns, a library could predict which books are likely to be in high demand and purchase additional copies in advance.

In addition to improving existing services, predictive analysis can also help libraries innovate and develop new services. For example, libraries could use predictive analysis to identify emerging research areas and develop new services to support them. Also, by predicting future trends in technology and information consumption, libraries could stay ahead of the curve and develop new digital services and resources.

Several libraries worldwide have already started using predictive analysis to enhance their services. For example, the University of Pennsylvania's Penn Libraries uses predictive analysis to forecast the demand for print and electronic resources. The Los Angeles Public Library uses predictive analysis to optimize its collection development and management.

However, implementing predictive analysis in library services is not without its challenges. Libraries need to have the necessary technical infrastructure and skills to collect, store, and analyze large amounts of data. They also need to ensure that they are using predictive analysis ethically and responsibly, respecting user privacy and data protection laws.

Despite these challenges, the potential benefits of predictive analysis for library services are too significant to ignore. By leveraging the power of AI and predictive analysis, libraries can not only enhance their existing services but also innovate and adapt to the rapidly changing information landscape. Predictive analysis represents an exciting new frontier for library services, promising a future where libraries are more responsive, efficient, and innovative than ever before.

In the age of AI, the traditional library is evolving into a dynamic, data-driven institution capable of anticipating and responding to user needs with unprecedented precision. As we delve deeper into this exciting era, predictive analysis will undoubtedly play a pivotal role in shaping the library of the future. The story of AI in library services is just beginning, and predictive analysis is set to be one of its most compelling chapters.

AI and Virtual Reality in Libraries

As we delve deeper into the realm of artificial intelligence, we find ourselves at the intersection of AI and virtual reality, particularly in the context of libraries. These two technological advancements, often considered the cornerstone of the fourth industrial revolution, are reshaping how libraries function and serve their patrons.

Artificial Intelligence, or AI, is often seen as a complex and intimidating concept, but at its core, it's simply a technology that enables machines to mimic human intelligence. AI has the potential to revolutionize library services in myriad ways. From automating routine tasks to providing personalized recommendations, AI can make library services more efficient and user-friendly.

Imagine walking into a library and being greeted by a virtual assistant who can guide you to the book you're looking for, suggest new reads based on your preferences, and even answer your queries about the library's services. This is no longer the stuff of science fiction, but a reality made possible by AI. AI-powered chatbots are increasingly being used in libraries to provide 24/7 customer service, answering frequently asked questions and guiding users through the library's resources.

AI can also be used to analyze user data to provide personalized recommendations. By analyzing a user's borrowing history and search patterns, AI can suggest books that align with their interests. This not only enhances the user experience but also increases the likelihood of users finding and borrowing books that they will enjoy.

Now, let's turn our attention to virtual reality (VR), another fascinating technology that's making its way into libraries. VR is a simulated experience that can be similar to or completely different from the real world. It can transport users to different places, times, and even fictional worlds, offering a level of immersion that traditional media cannot match.

Libraries are leveraging VR to transform the way users interact with their resources. For instance, VR can be used to create virtual tours of the library, allowing users to explore the library's resources and facilities from the comfort of their homes. This can be particularly useful for users with mobility issues or those who live far from the library.

Moreover, VR can also be used to enhance educational resources. Imagine being able to explore ancient ruins, walk on the surface of Mars, or dive into the depths of the ocean, all from the library. VR can make learning more engaging and interactive, thereby enriching the educational resources offered by libraries.

However, the integration of AI and VR in libraries is not without its challenges. Issues related to privacy, data security, and digital literacy need to be addressed. Furthermore, the cost of implementing these technologies can be a barrier for many libraries, especially those with limited budgets.

But despite these challenges, the potential benefits of AI and VR for libraries are immense. They can enhance library services, improve user experience, and even open up new avenues for learning and exploration. As we continue to navigate the digital age, libraries must embrace these technologies to stay relevant and meet the changing needs of their users.

Thus, the confluence of AI and VR is not just reshaping libraries, but also redefining what they can offer to their patrons. The future of libraries is here, and it is intelligent, immersive, and interactive.

AI in Library Space Design

As we venture further into the age of Artificial Intelligence (AI), it is becoming increasingly clear that this technology has the potential to revolutionize the world of library services. Not only can AI enhance the way we search for and access information, but it can also play a pivotal role in the design of library spaces.

Imagine stepping into a library where the physical layout and design have been optimized using AI algorithms. The bookshelves, seating areas, study rooms, and other resources are all placed in positions that maximize convenience, accessibility, and user satisfaction. This is not a far-fetched idea, but a reality that is already starting to take shape in some of the world's most forward-thinking libraries.

AI technology can analyze data from various sources, including user behavior, to create a library design that caters to the needs of its users. For instance, AI can track which sections of the library are most frequently visited, at what times, and by which demographic. This data can then be used to rearrange the library layout to improve traffic flow and user satisfaction.

Moreover, AI can be used to predict future trends and needs. By analyzing data from external sources, such as trends in publishing or education, AI can anticipate the resources that will be in high demand in the future. This can guide decisions about what materials to stock and where to place them in the library.

Intelligent systems can also assist in creating flexible and adaptable library spaces. As libraries are increasingly becoming more than just places to borrow books, spaces for collaborative work, community events, and digital media production are becoming more important. AI can help design these spaces by analyzing how they are used and suggesting improvements.

For example, AI could suggest changes to the layout of a computer lab based on usage data, or recommend the creation of a new meeting space based on the frequency of community events. In this way, AI becomes an invaluable tool for ensuring that library spaces continue to meet the evolving needs of their communities.

Furthermore, AI can be used to enhance the accessibility of library spaces. For individuals with disabilities, navigating a library can be a daunting task. AI can analyze the layout of a library and suggest changes that make it more accessible. This could include rearranging furniture to create clear paths, adjusting the height of bookshelves, or suggesting the installation of assistive technologies.

In terms of the environmental impact, AI can assist in creating more sustainable library spaces. By analyzing data on energy use, AI can suggest changes to lighting, heating, and cooling systems to reduce energy consumption. Additionally, AI can help design spaces that make better use of natural light and ventilation, contributing to a more sustainable and pleasant library environment.

In essence, the potential for AI in library space design is immense. It offers the ability to create library spaces that are more user-friendly, adaptable, accessible, and sustainable. As AI technology continues to advance, it's clear that it will play an increasingly important role in shaping the libraries of the future.

AI and the Evolution of Library Services

As the pages of time turn, libraries have continually evolved to meet the needs of their patrons. Once hallowed sanctuaries of silence, filled with towering stacks of books and card catalogs, they have transformed into dynamic, interactive spaces that incorporate digital resources and technology. Central to this evolution is the role of artificial intelligence (AI), a technological advancement that has the potential to greatly enhance library services.

AI's influence on library services is multifaceted. One of the most evident applications is in the sphere of data management. Libraries are treasure troves of information, comprising not just books, but academic journals, newspapers, multimedia, and digital resources. Organizing and managing this enormous volume of data is a herculean task. AI, with its proficiency in data analysis and management, steps into this role with ease. Machine learning algorithms can sort through vast amounts of data, categorizing and organizing them efficiently. This results in improved cataloging systems and efficient retrieval of information.

AI can also revolutionize the way libraries interact with their patrons. Virtual assistants, powered by AI, can provide 24/7 customer service, answering queries, assisting in information retrieval, and even recommending books based on a user's reading history. This not only enhances the user experience but also allows librarians to focus on more complex tasks that require human intervention.

AI's capability to predict trends can also be harnessed in library services. By analyzing borrowing patterns and user behavior, AI can help libraries anticipate future needs and preferences. This predictive analysis can guide decisions on acquisitions, resource allocation, and even library programming.

The implementation of AI also opens up new avenues for accessibility. Voice recognition and text-to-speech technologies can make library resources more accessible to patrons with disabilities. For instance, visually impaired users can utilize voice commands to search the library database, while text-to-speech can allow them to 'read' digital texts.

However, the integration of AI into library services is not without challenges. Concerns about data privacy and ethical use of AI are paramount. Libraries, as trusted institutions, have a responsibility to ensure that the use of AI respects user privacy and follows ethical guidelines. There is also the issue of keeping pace with rapidly evolving technology and ensuring that library staff are adequately trained to use and manage AI systems.

Moreover, while AI can augment library services, it cannot replace the human touch. Libraries are not just repositories of information, but also community spaces that foster human connection. The role of librarians in guiding, mentoring, and connecting with patrons remains vital. Thus, the goal should be to strike a balance, where AI enhances services without undermining the human-centric ethos of libraries.

The evolution of library services, driven by AI, is a testament to libraries' resilience and their commitment to serving the needs of their patrons. With careful planning and thoughtful implementation, AI can be a powerful tool in the library's arsenal, enabling them to provide more efficient, personalized, and inclusive services. As we turn the page to this new chapter in the story of libraries, it is clear that AI will be a key character, shaping the narrative and propelling libraries into the future.

Chapter 13: Building an AI-Ready Library

Developing an AI Strategy

As we delve into the realm of artificial intelligence, it's crucial to have a well-crafted strategy in place. The strategy will act as a roadmap, guiding libraries towards the successful implementation of AI technologies. It will help to identify the key areas where AI can enhance services, and highlight the steps necessary to realize these improvements.

The first step in developing this strategy is understanding the potential of AI. This means not only understanding the current capabilities of AI, but also being aware of its future possibilities. AI is a rapidly evolving field, and libraries must remain abreast of the latest developments to fully leverage its benefits. For instance, AI can help automate routine tasks, improve user interactions, and provide personalized recommendations, thereby enhancing the overall library experience for users.

Once the potential of AI is understood, the next step is to identify the specific areas within the library that can benefit from AI. This requires a thorough analysis of current library operations. The areas that are time-consuming, prone to errors, or can be improved in terms of user experience, are the ideal candidates for AI implementation.

After identifying the areas for AI implementation, it's time to plan the implementation process. This includes deciding on the AI technologies to be used, the changes to be made in the current operations, the staff training needed, and the metrics to measure the success of the implementation. It's important to remember that the implementation of AI is not a one-time process, but a continuous one. Therefore, the plan should also include regular reviews and updates to the AI systems.

While planning the implementation, it's also important to consider the ethical implications of using AI. Libraries, being trusted public institutions, have a responsibility to respect user privacy and ensure fair use of AI technologies. Therefore, the AI strategy should include guidelines to ensure ethical use of AI.

The next step in the strategy is to allocate resources for the AI implementation. This includes not only financial resources but also human resources. Libraries need to have staff members who are trained in AI technologies and can manage the AI systems. They may also need to hire external experts or collaborate with tech companies.

Finally, the strategy should include a comprehensive communication plan. This is important to manage the expectations of library users and staff. The communication plan should clearly convey the benefits of AI, address any concerns, and keep all stakeholders informed about the progress of the AI implementation.

Developing an AI strategy is a complex process that requires careful planning and execution. However, the rewards can be significant. AI has the potential to transform library services, making them more efficient, personalized, and user-friendly. With a well-crafted strategy, libraries can harness the power of AI to enhance their services and provide a better experience for their users.

The journey of AI implementation in libraries is just beginning, and the possibilities are immense. By developing a robust AI strategy, libraries can ensure they are on the right path to harness the full potential of AI.

Building an AI-Ready Infrastructure

Once upon a time, in the heart of a bustling city, there was a grand library. This library was a treasure trove of knowledge, brimming with books, documents, and digital resources. However, the library was also facing a challenge. The volume of information was growing exponentially, and the librarians were struggling to manage and organize it efficiently.

Recognizing the need for a solution, the library's head librarian, Ms. Eleanor, decided to employ cutting-edge technology. She knew that Artificial Intelligence (AI), with its ability to process vast amounts of data quickly and accurately, could be the key to enhancing the library's services.

The first step towards this transformative journey was to build an AI-ready infrastructure. Eleanor knew that this was no small task. It required careful planning, adequate resources, and the right expertise. But she was determined to harness the power of AI for the library's betterment.

The library's existing infrastructure was traditional and largely manual. Eleanor realized that to integrate AI, the library needed a robust and flexible digital infrastructure. This would allow for the seamless integration of AI tools and applications, and the efficient handling of large data volumes.

The library started by investing in high-performance computing systems capable of processing large amounts of data. These systems were equipped with powerful processors and ample storage space. The library also adopted cloud services for scalability and flexibility, allowing it to handle peak data loads without any disruption in service.

Next, the library needed a reliable network infrastructure. A high-speed, secure network was crucial for fast data transmission and real-time AI applications. It also facilitated remote access to library resources, a feature that had become increasingly important in the digital age.

Data was the lifeblood of AI, and the library had plenty of it. However, it was essential to organize and structure this data for effective AI utilization. The library adopted data management tools for data cleaning, integration, and standardization. It also implemented data security measures to safeguard user privacy and data integrity.

The library also recognized the importance of AI software and algorithms. It explored various AI technologies like machine learning, natural language processing, and predictive analytics. These technologies would enable the library to provide personalized recommendations, automate routine tasks, and predict future trends.

Staff training was another critical aspect of the AI-ready infrastructure. The library staff needed to understand AI and its implications. They also needed to learn how to use AI tools effectively. The library organized training sessions and workshops, equipping its staff with the necessary skills and knowledge.

The library also established partnerships with tech companies and academic institutions. These partnerships provided the library with technical expertise and resources. They also facilitated research and development in AI and library science.

Building an AI-ready infrastructure was a challenging yet rewarding endeavor. It involved technical upgrades, staff training, data management, and strategic partnerships. But the library was committed to this journey. It believed that AI could revolutionize library services, making them more efficient, personalized, and accessible.

The story of this library serves as an inspiration for other libraries. It demonstrates that with the right infrastructure, planning, and resources, AI can be a powerful tool for enhancing library services. It shows that libraries, traditional guardians of knowledge, can also be pioneers of technological innovation.

Creating a Culture of Innovation

In the realm of libraries, as in any other field, innovation is not a one-time event. It is a culture, a habit, a way of life. It is a continuous process that requires constant nurturing and fostering. The key to this is creating an environment that not only welcomes but also encourages new and creative ideas. This culture of innovation is integral to the use of AI in enhancing library services.

To foster this culture, it is essential to start with a change in mindset. Libraries are not just repositories of books and knowledge but can also be hubs of innovation and creativity. The traditional view of the library as a quiet, static place needs to be replaced with a dynamic, interactive, and innovative image. This means not just incorporating AI and other technologies but also rethinking the role of libraries and librarians in the digital age.

In this culture, librarians are no longer just custodians of books but become innovators and facilitators. They are the ones who can leverage AI to create new services, improve existing ones, and provide a better user experience. They can use AI to analyze user behavior, predict trends, and make recommendations. They can use AI to automate routine tasks, freeing them up to focus on more strategic and creative tasks.

Creating this culture requires not just a change in mindset but also a change in practices and policies. It requires creating spaces for experimentation and learning. It requires providing resources and training for librarians to learn about AI and other technologies. It requires encouraging collaboration and knowledge sharing. It requires recognizing and rewarding innovation.

One way to foster this culture is through hackathons and innovation competitions. These events can bring together librarians, technologists, and users to brainstorm and prototype new ideas. They can provide a platform for showcasing and testing new technologies. They can also provide an opportunity for librarians to learn from each other and from experts in the field.

Another way is through partnerships and collaborations. Libraries can partner with technology companies, universities, and other organizations to gain access to expertise and resources. They can collaborate with other libraries to share knowledge and best practices. They can also collaborate with users to understand their needs and co-create solutions.

Creating a culture of innovation also requires leadership. Leaders need to set the vision and direction. They need to create an environment that encourages risk-taking and tolerates failure. They need to champion innovation and lead by example.

But creating a culture of innovation is not enough. It also needs to be sustained. This requires continuous learning and improvement. It requires keeping up with the latest trends and technologies. It requires evaluating and measuring the impact of innovations. It requires celebrating successes and learning from failures.

In the context of AI, creating a culture of innovation is not just about using AI to enhance library services. It is also about using AI to drive innovation. AI can be a tool for innovation, providing insights and capabilities that were not possible before. But it can also be a catalyst for innovation, inspiring new ideas and approaches.

In the end, creating a culture of innovation is about more than just technology. It is about people, processes, and mindset. It is about transforming libraries from passive repositories of knowledge to active hubs of innovation. And it is about leveraging AI to make this transformation possible.

Engaging Stakeholders in AI Implementation

As we delve further into the integration of AI in library services, it is imperative to consider the involvement of all stakeholders. These include the library staff, patrons, management, and even the wider community. Their engagement is crucial in ensuring the successful implementation of AI.

The first step towards this is creating awareness about AI and its potential benefits. This involves dispelling misconceptions and fears about AI and automation, especially the fear of job losses among library staff. It's essential to communicate that AI is not meant to replace humans but rather to augment their capabilities and free them from routine tasks. This will allow the staff to focus on more complex and creative tasks, thereby enhancing their job satisfaction and productivity.

Once the staff understands the benefits of AI, they are more likely to support its adoption. Training programs can be initiated to equip them with the necessary skills to use AI tools effectively. These programs can be designed in a way that encourages active participation and hands-on experience, making the learning process more enjoyable and effective.

The next group of stakeholders to engage is the library patrons. They are the primary beneficiaries of AI-enhanced library services. Therefore, their needs and expectations should be taken into account during the AI implementation process. Feedback mechanisms can be established to gather their opinions and suggestions. This can be done through surveys, focus group discussions, or informal conversations.

The library management also plays a crucial role in the AI implementation process. Their support is needed in terms of providing the necessary resources and creating an enabling environment for AI adoption. They need to understand the value of AI in improving library services and the return on investment it promises. This can be achieved through presentations, reports, and demonstrations of successful AI implementations in other libraries.

Lastly, the wider community should not be left out. Libraries are community resources and their services have a direct impact on the community's well-being. Therefore, the community's understanding and acceptance of AI are crucial. Public forums can be organized to introduce AI and its benefits. The community can also be invited to participate in the library's AI projects, such as contributing to data collection or testing new AI tools.

The engagement of stakeholders should not stop at the implementation phase. It should be an ongoing process, with regular updates and feedback sessions. This will ensure that the AI tools are continuously improved to meet the evolving needs of the users.

To sum it up, the implementation of AI in libraries is not just a technical process but also a social one. It requires the active involvement and support of all stakeholders. By engaging them effectively, libraries can harness the power of AI to enhance their services and create a better experience for their users.

Chapter 14: Conclusion: The Transformative Potential of AI in Libraries

Recap: AI and Libraries

In the quiet, hallowed halls of libraries, a soft hum of transformation resonates. The world of libraries, often associated with dusty shelves and silence, is experiencing a revolution. This revolution is not loud or disruptive but is instead marked by an intelligent, invisible force that is subtly reshaping the way libraries function and serve their communities. This force is none other than Artificial Intelligence (AI).

AI, with its ability to process vast amounts of data and learn from it, is a tool that is revolutionizing various sectors, and libraries are no exception. It is vital to understand that AI does not aim to replace human librarians but to enhance their capabilities, making them more efficient and effective in their roles. This technology can handle repetitive tasks, freeing up librarians to focus on higher-level tasks that require human judgment and creativity.

The introduction of AI in libraries has brought about significant changes in cataloging and classification processes. Traditional methods of classification, such as the Dewey Decimal System, have been labor-intensive and time-consuming. AI, with its ability to recognize patterns and analyze data, can automate these processes, making them faster and more accurate. This not only saves time but also enhances the user experience by making it easier to find relevant materials.

AI is also transforming the way libraries manage their collections. Predictive analytics, a branch of AI, can analyze data on book loans and returns to predict future demand for certain titles. This allows libraries to manage their collections more effectively, ensuring that popular titles are always available while minimizing the space wasted on less popular books.

The impact of AI is also felt in the way libraries interact with their users. Chatbots, powered by AI, are now common features on library websites. These chatbots can answer simple queries, guide users through the website, and even help them find the books they are looking for. Moreover, AI can provide personalized recommendations based on a user's reading history, enhancing the user experience and encouraging more usage of library resources.

AI's role in libraries extends beyond just operational efficiency. It is also a powerful tool for accessibility. AI technologies can convert text to speech, making written materials accessible to visually impaired users. Similarly, AI can translate text into different languages, breaking down language barriers and making library resources accessible to a wider audience.

However, the integration of AI into libraries is not without challenges. Data privacy and security are significant concerns. Libraries have always been custodians of their users' privacy, and the use of AI must respect this tradition. Ethical use of AI, which respects user privacy while providing enhanced services, is a delicate balancing act that libraries must master.

Moreover, the successful integration of AI in libraries requires investment in infrastructure and training. Libraries need to have the necessary hardware and software to support AI technologies. Librarians need to be trained to use these technologies effectively and to understand the ethical implications of their use.

Despite these challenges, the potential benefits of AI for libraries are immense. By harnessing the power of AI, libraries can become more efficient, more accessible, and more responsive to their users' needs. The quiet revolution of AI in libraries is just beginning, and its impact will be felt for years to come.

The Promise of AI for Libraries

As we delve deeper into the fascinating world of artificial intelligence, its potential for transforming libraries becomes increasingly evident. Imagine a world where AI-powered systems can predict what resources a library user may need even before they do. Or where intelligent systems can help librarians manage, categorize, and recommend resources with unprecedented accuracy and efficiency. This is not a distant dream, but rather the very real promise that AI holds for libraries.

Libraries have always been gateways to knowledge, providing users with access to a vast array of information. However, the sheer volume of resources can sometimes be overwhelming, making it difficult for users to find exactly what they need. AI has the potential to revolutionize this aspect of library services. Through advanced algorithms and machine learning, AI can analyze a user's past searches and preferences to recommend resources that align with their interests and needs. This personalized approach not only enhances the user's experience but also increases the utility and relevance of the library's resources.

AI can also streamline the management of library resources. Cataloging and organizing resources is a time-consuming task that requires significant manual effort. AI can automate these tasks, freeing up librarians to focus on more strategic activities. For instance, AI-powered systems can analyze the content of books and other resources to categorize them accurately. They can also identify patterns and trends in resource usage, allowing libraries to optimize their collections based on user demand.

The promise of AI for libraries extends beyond resource management and user services. AI can also help libraries become more inclusive and accessible. For example, AI-powered speech recognition and text-to-speech technologies can make library resources accessible to users with visual impairments or literacy challenges. Similarly, AI can help libraries reach out to non-English speakers by providing translation services.

Moreover, AI can help libraries become more proactive in their outreach. By analyzing user data, AI can predict trends and identify opportunities for engagement. For instance, if a user frequently borrows books on a particular topic, the library could recommend related events or workshops. This proactive approach not only enhances the user's experience but also fosters a deeper connection between the library and its users.

However, realizing the promise of AI for libraries is not without challenges. Libraries must navigate issues related to data privacy and ethical use of AI. They must also invest in the necessary infrastructure and training. Despite these challenges, the potential benefits of AI make it a worthwhile pursuit for libraries.

The promise of AI for libraries is not just about enhancing services or improving efficiency. It's about reimagining what libraries can be in the digital age. With AI, libraries can become more than just repositories of information. They can become personalized learning hubs, inclusive community centers, and proactive providers of knowledge. The journey towards this future may be complex and challenging, but it's a journey worth taking. For in the end, the promise of AI for libraries is the promise of a better, more inclusive, and more engaging library experience for all.

Preparing for the AI-Driven Future

As we turn the page and delve into the uncharted territory of artificial intelligence (AI), it is crucial to understand that this isn't just another technological trend. It is a transformative force, like fire or the wheel, that holds the potential to reshape our world in ways we can only begin to imagine. Libraries, as the guardians of knowledge and information, are uniquely positioned to harness the power of AI to enhance their services and better serve their patrons.

To prepare for the AI-driven future, it is essential to understand the technology's potential and its implications. AI is not merely a tool for automating mundane tasks. It is a sophisticated technology capable of learning, adapting, and making decisions. It can analyze vast amounts of data, identify patterns, and generate insights that would be impossible for humans to discern. This ability can be harnessed to enhance library services in numerous ways, from improving resource management and discovery to personalizing user experiences and expanding access to knowledge.

However, embracing AI is not without challenges. Libraries must navigate complex issues around data privacy, ethical use of AI, and the digital divide. Moreover, implementing AI requires significant investment in infrastructure, skills, and resources. Libraries must therefore approach AI with a strategic mindset, considering both its potential benefits and its potential risks.

One way libraries can prepare for the AI-driven future is by developing a comprehensive AI strategy. This should outline the library's goals for AI, the resources it will allocate to AI initiatives, and the measures it will take to mitigate risks. The strategy should also include plans for staff training and development, as AI will require new skills and competencies.

Libraries should also cultivate partnerships and collaborations to leverage AI. This could involve partnering with technology companies, academic institutions, or other libraries to share resources, expertise, and best practices. Collaborations can also help libraries stay abreast of the latest developments in AI and ensure they are using the technology in the most effective and ethical manner.

Moreover, libraries must advocate for fair and ethical use of AI. They should engage in policy discussions and advocate for regulations that protect user privacy, promote transparency, and ensure equitable access to AI benefits. Libraries have a unique role to play in promoting digital literacy and helping patrons understand and navigate the complexities of the AI-driven world.

As we move towards the AI-driven future, it is clear that libraries have a crucial role to play. They are not just passive observers of the AI revolution, but active participants shaping its trajectory. By understanding the potential of AI, developing strategic plans, fostering collaborations, and advocating for ethical use of AI, libraries can ensure they are ready for the opportunities and challenges that lie ahead.

The AI-driven future is not a distant reality, but a present possibility. Libraries, with their commitment to knowledge, learning, and service, are well-equipped to navigate this brave new world. By embracing AI, they can enhance their services, enrich their patrons' experiences, and contribute to a more informed, inclusive, and enlightened society. The future is AI, and libraries are ready to lead the way.

Final Thoughts

As we conclude our exploration of the potential of AI in enhancing library services, it's essential to take a step back and reflect on our journey thus far. It's been an enlightening voyage, traversing the landscape of artificial intelligence and its integration into the library ecosystem. We've witnessed the transformative power of AI, its capacity to revolutionize library services, and the challenges it presents.

Artificial intelligence is not just a tool; it's a partner in the process of knowledge dissemination. It has the potential to redefine the role of libraries in our societies and the services they provide. From automating tedious tasks to personalizing user experiences, AI has demonstrated its capacity to improve efficiency and user satisfaction in libraries.

However, as with any transformative technology, AI also brings challenges. These include ethical considerations, data privacy issues, and the need for technical expertise. It is crucial for libraries to navigate these challenges carefully, balancing the benefits of AI with the potential risks. This includes ensuring transparency in AI systems, protecting user data, and investing in staff training.

In this context, it is worth noting that AI is not meant to replace humans in libraries. Instead, it should be seen as an enabler, a tool that can help librarians provide better services. It can take over repetitive tasks, freeing librarians to focus on more complex and creative aspects of their work. This includes building relationships with users, curating collections, and fostering a love for learning and knowledge.

Moreover, AI can help libraries stay relevant in the digital age. It can help them adapt to changing user needs and expectations, providing personalized, on-demand services. It can also help libraries reach out to new users, breaking down barriers to access and participation.

While the potential of AI in libraries is vast, it is important to remember that its implementation should be guided by the mission and values of libraries. This includes upholding principles such as intellectual freedom, equal access to information, and respect for user privacy. AI should be used to enhance these principles, not undermine them.

The integration of AI into library services is a journey, not a destination. It requires continuous learning, experimentation, and adaptation. It also requires collaboration between libraries, technology providers, and users. Together, they can shape the future of libraries, ensuring that they remain vibrant, inclusive, and essential spaces in our societies.

As we look to the future, it's clear that AI will play a pivotal role in libraries. It's a journey that's just beginning, and we're excited to see where it will lead. We hope this book has provided you with insights, inspiration, and practical guidance on how to leverage AI in your library. Remember, the goal is not to 'robotize' your library, but to use AI as a tool to enhance your services, meet user needs, and fulfill your mission.

So here we stand at the crossroads of an exciting future, where AI and libraries converge. Let's move forward together, with curiosity, courage, and commitment, to create libraries that are not just repositories of knowledge, but catalysts for learning, innovation, and community building. Let's harness the power of AI to create libraries that are more efficient, user-friendly, and inclusive. Let's create libraries that truly serve the needs and aspirations of our users, our communities, and our societies.

References

Abrams, M., Abrams, J., Cullen, P., & Goldstein, L. (2019). Artificial Intelligence, Ethics, and Enhanced Data Stewardship. *IEEE Security & Privacy*, *17*(2), 17–30. https://doi.org/10.1109/msec.2018.2888778

Advancing Cognitive Accessibility: The Role of Artificial Intelligence in Enhancing Inclusivity. (2024). *PriMera Scientific Engineering*. https://doi.org/10.56831/psen-04-108

Ahmadikia, A. A., Shirzad, A., & Saghiri, A. M. (2024). A Bibliometric Analysis of Quantum Machine Learning Research. *Science & Technology Libraries*, 1–22. https://doi.org/10.1080/0194262x.2023.2292049

AI Lab. (2023). The University of Rhode Island's AI Lab. Retrieved March 4, 2024, from https://web.uri.edu/ai/

Aithal, S., & Aithal, P. S. (2023). Effects of AI-Based ChatGPT on Higher Education Libraries. *International Journal of Management, Technology, and Social Sciences*, 95–108. https://doi.org/10.47992/ijmts.2581.6012.0272

Aken, R. A. (1986). Directory of automated library systems. *Information Processing & Management*, *22*(6), 555. https://doi.org/10.1016/0306-4573(86)90112-3

Ali, M. Y., Naeem, S. B., & Bhatti, R. (2020). Artificial intelligence tools and perspectives of university librarians: An overview. *Business Information Review*, *37*(3), 116–124. https://doi.org/10.1177/0266382120952016

Allison, D. (2012). Chatbots in the library: is it time? *Library Hi Tech*, *30*(1), 95–107. https://doi.org/10.1108/07378831211213238

www.ingramcontent.com/pod-product-compliance
Lightning Source LLC
LaVergne TN
LVHW022124060326
832903LV00063B/3634